STUDY GUIDE II
A WORKBOOK TO ACCOMPANY

❖❖❖❖❖

BARON

PSYCHOLOGY

THIRD EDITION

Robin Hailstorks
Prince George's Community College

Robert Osterhouse
Prince George's Community College

Alan Schultz
Prince George's Community College

Mary Helen Spear
Prince George's Community College

Marilynn Thomas
Prince George's Community College

Allyn and Bacon
Boston · London · Toronto · Sydney · Tokyo · Singapore

ISBN 0-205-17418-3

Printed in the United States of America

10 9 8 7 6 5 4   00 99 98 97

PREFACE

The development of this unique student workbook began as a response to our students' need for more structure. Developed initially as an integral component of the PSI or self-paced course, a few editions ago, we soon found that faculty were including the workbook and objectives in their more traditional courses as well.

By providing a clear statement of the specific material students will be held responsible for, the objectives provide practice in extracting information from the text, allow students to process that information in a way that aids them in developing and writing their own ideas, and leave them with an organized document to study and review from for tests.

One of the most important aspects of this workbook is the level of specificity of the learning objectives, which attempt to narrow down, consolidate and integrate the immense quantity of information found in introductory psychology textbooks. We have found that detailed, clearly written learning objectives are of greater value to the student than the more general objectives often seen in other workbooks. To make it more user friendly, each objective is followed by a page number which relates it to the textbook, and the amount of space provided for the answer is related to the length of the expected outcome.

Another important aspect is the active involvement on the part of students who complete the work on their own rather than reviewing from a written out summary. At the completion of each chapter, students should have a summary of the important concepts in their own words. The objectives outline, in some respect, all of the material the student is required to master and retain. This dovetails nicely with expected course outcomes.

The importance of learning objectives in the self-paced course is paramount. As the professor does not lecture on a regular basis, students must have a clear idea of which concepts and information are essential to the course. With this workbook, whatever the teaching modality, the instructor retains flexibility to change course content by assigning the relevant learning objective numbers.

Student response to the objectives and to the workbook has been quite favorable. They seem particularly to appreciate the structure inherent in this system -- in that they know precisely what material they are expected to have mastered. Faculty have been appreciative of the flexibility it affords them to include or exclude whatever information they choose -- simply by identifying the objective numbers.

We hope this workbook will help other students be more successful in studying psychology. We also welcome your feedback on this approach.

TO THE STUDENT

This workbook contains some unique features which will help you in learning the material.

♦ Workbook questions help you focus on most of the essential content in each chapter.

♦ Each chapter is followed by a self-test.

 ♦ The answer key for the self-test is at the end of the book.

 ♦ The self-test samples your knowledge once you have filled out the questions. Each question on the self-test is followed by a number in parentheses ( ), which refers by number to a question you have filled out in the chapter.

♦ Sections of the chapter are separated by the same headings you will find in the text. Be aware of how the questions in each section are related to each other.

♦ Some questions have information given in the stem of the question. You are responsible for that information as well as the information from the text.

♦ The nature of the questions in the workbook varies with the material.

 ♦ Some of the questions are factual, i.e. they require you to copy information straight from the text.

 ♦ Other questions require you to find essential information and then interact with it in some way, i.e. to summarize the differences or similarities between two theories.

 ♦ You will find some charts which will help you organize essential information in meaningful ways, aiding recall.

TABLE OF CONTENTS

CHAPTER 1   PSYCHOLOGY 1

CHAPTER 2   BIOLOGICAL BASES OF BEHAVIOR 11

CHAPTER 3   SENSATION AND PERCEPTION 23

CHAPTER 4   CONSCIOUSNESS 35

CHAPTER 5   LEARNING 49

CHAPTER 6   MEMORY 59

CHAPTER 7   COGNITION 71

CHAPTER 8   HUMAN DEVELOPMENT I 85

CHAPTER 9   HUMAN DEVELOPMENT II 97

CHAPTER 10   MOTIVATION AND EMOTION 113

CHAPTER 11   INDIVIDUAL DIFFERENCES I 125

CHAPTER 12   INDIVIDUAL DIFFERENCES II 139

CHAPTER 13   HEALTH, STRESS, AND COPING 151

CHAPTER 14   PSYCHOLOGICAL DISORDERS 163

CHAPTER 15   THERAPY 177

CHAPTER 16   SOCIAL THOUGHT AND SOCIAL BEHAVIOR 189

CHAPTER 17   PSYCHOLOGY GOES TO WORK: 205

APPENDIX   STATISTICS 219

               ANSWER KEY 226

CHAPTER 1

PSYCHOLOGY:
ITS NATURE, SCOPE, AND METHODS

PSYCHOLOGY: WHAT IT IS AND HOW IT DEVELOPED

1. Define psychology. (3)

    List three psychology topics you are interested in learning more about in this course. (see Table 1.1)

    a.

    b.

    c.

2. The field of psychology has its roots in the disciplines of philosophy, biology, and physiology. Major developments in these disciplines served as a foundation for scientific psychology. To better understand how psychologists have defined the field, contrast the early views of the three major figures in the history of the field listed below. Also list the school of psychological thought with which they were associated. (4-6; also see page 6, key people in psychology).

    a.   Wilhelm Wundt
         1) school of psychological thought

         2) early views

    b.   William James
         1) school of psychological thought

         2) early views

    c.   J.B.Watson
         1) school of psychological thought

         2) early views

1

3.   The field of psychology developed greatly during the 20th century. Describe the major developments of the field during the following decades. (6-7)

   a.   1950s

   b.   1960s

   c.   1970s and 1980s

4.   The modern view of psychology suggests that there are key perspectives for examining behavior in the broadest sense of the term. Describe the focus or major interests of the following perspectives in psychology and provide an example of each perspective as well. (7-12; and see Table 1.2)

   a.   behavioral perspective

          example:

   b.   cognitive perspective

          example:

   c.   psychodynamic perspective

          example:

   d.   humanistic perspective

          example:

   e.   biopsychological perspective

          example:

      f.   evolutionary perspective

            example:

      g.   sociocultural perspective

            example:

5.   Describe how the multicultural perspective in psychology influenced guidelines for providing psychological services to culturally diverse populations. (13)

6.   Some people believe that psychology is not a science in the same sense as chemistry or physics. Describe what the word science actually means. Include in your answer the two aspects of methods. (15)

     Based on this definition, is psychology really a science? (15)

     Describe why common sense isn't quite as useful a guide to human behavior as it seems. (15)

PSYCHOLOGY: WHO AND WHAT

7.   List the academic degree awarded and describe the difference in training between a psychiatrist and a psychologist. (16-17)

      a.   psychiatrists (MD)

    b.   psychologists (   )

8.   List the major subfield of psychology that would study or investigate each of the following aspects of behavior. (17-18; and see Figure 1.4)

    a.   _____ studies all aspects of social behavior and social thought.

    b.   _____ studies all aspects of behavior in work settings.

    c.   _____ studies all aspects of basic psychological processes such as perception, learning, and motivation.

    d.   _____ studies how people change physically, cognitively, and socially over the entire lifespan.

    e.   _____ investigates all aspects of cognition - memory, thinking, reasoning, etc.

    f.   _____ studies all aspects of the educational process.

    g.   _____ investigates the biological bases of behavior.

    h.   _____ assists individuals in dealing with many personal problems that do not involve psychological disorders.

    i.   _____ studies the diagnosis, causes, and treatment of mental disorders.

ADDING TO WHAT WE KNOW:
THE PROCESS OF PSYCHOLOGICAL RESEARCH

9.   Describe how data about behavior is gathered through naturalistic observation. (19-20)

    Describe one reason that data gathered by this method may have reduced scientific value. (20)

    Describe one advantage of this kind of data. (20)

10.   Data about behavior can be gathered by using the case study method, in which detailed information is gathered about a specific individual. List one obvious drawback of using case studies as a means to develop general principles about human behavior. (20)

11.   Describe how data about behavior is gathered in the survey approach. (20-21)

        List two advantages of surveys. (21)

        a.

        b.

        List two disadvantages to gathering data through surveys. (21)

        a.

        b.

12.   Define the correlational method of research as a technique for determining the relationship between two events or two variables. (21-22)

        List three advantages of the correlational method of research. (22)

        a.

        b.

        c.

        Describe one major limitation of the correlational method of research that may lessen its appeal, at least to a degree. (22)

Give your own example (not one from the text) of a correlation between two events which does not imply causation. (22-23; and see Table 1.3)

13.   Define experimentation. (23)

Describe why experimentation is frequently the research method of choice for psychologists. (23-24)

List the two basic steps of the experimental method. (24)

a.

b.

Define the following two terms which are part of the experimental method. (24)

independent variable

dependent variable

Describe two conditions which must be met before experimentation can be used to describe the causes of a certain behavior. (24-25)

a.

b.

Describe how experimenter effects and demand characteristics can inadvertently lead to incorrect conclusions regarding the cause of a certain behavior in an experiment. (26-27)

a.

b.

Describe how the double-blind procedure can be used to eliminate the possibility of experimenter effects and demand characteristics. (27)

14.   Once a research study has been completed, a psychologist must interpret the results. One useful tool to accomplish this is called inferential statistics. Describe what kind of information inferential statistics can provide to the researcher. (27)

15.   Define meta-analysis. (29)

16.   Theories represent efforts by scientists in any field to answer the question "Why?". Theories consists of two major parts: (1) basic concepts and (2) statements concerning relationships between these concepts. Describe the critical process that begins once a theory has been formulated. (31; and see Figure 1.7)

ETHICAL ISSUES IN PSYCHOLOGICAL RESEARCH

17.   One ethical question regarding research has to do with the deception of research subjects - cases in which subjects have information about the purpose of the study withheld or are provided misleading information about the purpose. Describe why deception has sometimes been used in psychological research. (32)

        List and describe two conditions which must be present in a research study if any deception of subjects takes place. (33)

        a.

        b.

18.   The use of animals in research has recently generated a great deal of controversy. Many psychologists believe that it is appropriate to conduct at least some research projects with animals. Describe the potential benefits of using animals in psychological research. (33-35)

19.   Describe two ethical dilemmas that may be experienced by psychologists in private practice. (35-36)

a.

b.

USING THE KNOWLEDGE IN THIS BOOK:
SOME TIPS ON HOW TO STUDY

21.   List the six concrete tips on how to get the most out of the time you spend studying.

a.

b.

c.

d.

e.

f.

CHAPTER ONE QUIZ

1. Who started the school of functionalism arguing that the goal of psychology was to determine how the mind allowed us to adapt to a changing world? (2)

    a. Wilhelm Wundt
    b. John Watson
    c. Sigmund Freud
    d. William James

2. The current perspective that studies thinking, memory, and problem solving strategies is called the _____ perspective. (4)

    a. psychodynamic
    b. cognitive
    c. social-cultural
    d. physiological

3. Compared to scientific psychology, common sense psychology is: (6)
    a. usually just as accurate
    b. more skeptical
    c. often more contradictory
    d. as listed in all the other alternatives

4. Jan is a psychologist who knows a lot about interactions with other people. Her specialty is most likely to be: (8)

    a. clinical psychology
    b. industrial/organizational psychology
    c. experimental psychology
    d. social psychology

5. Freud based his ideas about human personality on extensive interviews with his clients. He had them tell him about their lives, especially their early childhood experiences. Freud's method of obtaining this information is called: (10)

    a. an experiment
    b. naturalistic observation
    c. a case method
    d. systematic desensitization

6. Which of the following is a limitation of the correlational method? (12)

    a. It can not be used to determine cause and effect relationships
    b. It can not be employed in naturalistic settings
    c. only a limited number and type of variables can be studied
    d. all of the other alternatives are limitations of this research method

7.   Andy wants to do research that will give information about the explanation goal of psychology. His method should be: (13)

      a.   naturalistic observation
      b.   correlation
      c.   experimentation
      d.   all of the other alternatives are correct

8.   A special branch of mathematics designed, in part, to evaluate the likelihood that a given pattern of findings is due to chance is called _____ statistics. (14)

      a.   descriptive
      b.   confirmation
      c.   random
      d.   inferential

9.   Confidence in a theory is improved when: (16)

      a.   greater numbers of psychologists find the theory attractive
      b.   hypotheses based on the theory are confirmed in research
      c.   best-selling books are based on the theory
      d.   a theory does not lend itself to further modification

10.   Deception in experiments has to do with: (17)

      a.   faking experimental findings in order to be published
      b.   subjects providing false information about themselves
      c.   withholding information from subjects so that their behavior is unaffected
      d.   statistically significant results that are invalid

CHAPTER 2

BIOLOGICAL BASES OF BEHAVIOR:
A LOOK BENEATH THE SURFACE

1. Define biopsychology. List four questions that the field of biopsychology might attempt answering. (46)

    a.

    b.

    c.

    d.

2. Neurons are the cells of the nervous system. They are found throughout the nervous system in various shapes and sizes. Describe the functions of the following parts of the neuron. (47)

    a. dendrites

    b. axon

    c. myelin sheath

    d. axon terminals

    e. synapse

3. Describe the process of communication within the neuron. Include and underline the following terms: action potential, resting potential, all-or-none response. (47-49)

4.   Describe synaptic transmission, the process of communication between neurons. Be sure to include, underline, and describe the terms synaptic vesicles and neurotransmitters. (49-51) (Note: the synapse and synaptic gap are the same)

5.   Describe the function of the two important neurotransmitters listed below. (52-53)

   a.   acetylcholine

   b.   endorphins

   How do the following drugs affect synaptic transmission? (54-55)

   a.   cocaine and amphetamines

   b.   opiates

THE NERVOUS SYSTEM: ITS BASIC STRUCTURE AND FUNCTION

6.   The nervous system is divided and subdivided into several parts. If you look over the chart which follows you will be better able to understand the organization of the divisions. Describe the functions of the following parts of the nervous system: (55-57)

   a.   spinal cord

   b.   somatic nervous system

c.   autonomic nervous system

d.   sympathetic nervous system

e.   parasympathetic nervous system

Complete the following chart. (56)

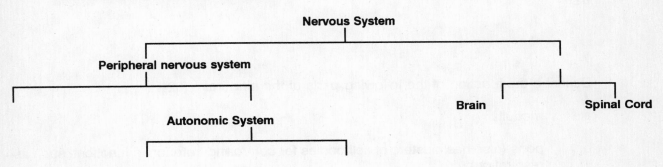

7.   Biopsychologists studying the nervous system have devised a number of techniques for investigating the functioning brain. You have probably heard of several of these techniques because they are used in medicine for diagnostic purposes. Describe the following techniques or procedures. (59-60)

a.   electroencephalography or EEG

b.   SQUID

c.   MRI

d.   PET

THE BRAIN: WHERE CONSCIOUSNESS DWELLS

8.   If you have heard of individuals "chug-a-lugging" a quart of alcohol and dying from it you have seen what alcohol does to one part of the brain--the medulla. The hindbrain, the part of your brain just above your spinal cord at the base of your head contains several structures which are critical to keeping you alive and awake. Describe the brainstem. (61-62)

Describe the function of the following parts of the hindbrain. (62)

a.   medulla

b.   pons (also has clusters of cell bodies for controlling autonomic functions such as respiration)

c.   reticular activating system (a diffuse bunch of fibers also referred to as the reticular formation) - also linked to attention, including attention deficit disorder

d.   cerebellum

9.   Deep within our brains are centers for appetites, emotions and motives. Describe the functions of the following structures in our brain. (62-64)

a.   hypothalamus

      b.   thalamus

      c.   limbic system

10.   The cerebral cortex controls most of the activities which we view as uniquely human--such as problem solving and speech. Describe the cerebral cortex, and the functions of the four lobes or divisions of each hemisphere. (64-65)

      a.   cerebral cortex

      b.   frontal lobes

      c.   parietal lobes

      d.   occipital lobes

      e.   temporal lobes

11.   Label the indicated <u>four lobes of the brain</u>, the <u>primary somatic projection area</u> (somatosensory cortex), and the <u>motor cortex</u>. (65)

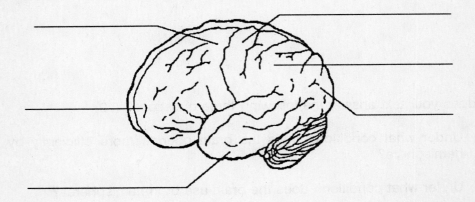

LATERALIZATION OF THE CEREBRAL CORTEX:
TWO MINDS IN ONE BODY.

12.   Define lateralization and describe how lateralization of function is related to speech. (68)

a.   lateralization

b.   relationship to speech

Each hemisphere of the brain seems to be specialized for somewhat different tasks. List five specialized functions that appear to be controlled by the left hemisphere. (68)

a.

b.

c.

d.

e.

List three specialized functions that appear to be controlled by the right hemisphere. (68)

a.

b.

c.

13.   After reading about the experiments describing the effect of cutting the corpus callosum, determine the function of the corpus callosum. (70-71)

14.   How does your text answer the following three questions? (72)

a.   Under what conditions does the brain operate more efficiently by using one hemisphere?

b.   Under what conditions does the brain use both hemispheres?

c.   Can you do two things at once?

THE ENDOCRINE SYSTEM:
CHEMICAL REGULATORS OF BODILY PROCESSES

15.   You have heard of hormones and already know how many of them function. In this chapter your text looks specifically at neurohormones which affect the nervous system. How do neurohormones differ from neurotransmitters? (73)

a.

b.

c.

d.

16.   Hormones secreted by the sex glands or gonads have a powerful effect on cognitive, social and physical development. Describe two syndromes which are the result of the system malfunctioning. (74)

a.

b.

HEREDITY AND BEHAVIOR

17.   Define the following terms: (78 - do not use the definitions in the margin)

a.   chromosomes

b.   genes

c.   DNA

18.   What issues or information can the study of identical twins raised apart clarify? (79-80)

       What did a 1989 study concerning twins and job satisfaction conclude? (80)

THE RESEARCH PROCESS

19.   Describe the following studies which explored whether sexual orientation could be genetically determined. (80-82)

       a.   LeVay, 1991

       b.   Bailey and Pillard, 1991 (see figure 2.14)

       c.   Hamer et al., 1993

MAKING PSYCHOLOGY A PART OF YOUR LIFE

20.   Define Traumatic Brain Injury. (83-84)

List three common features of TBI patients.

a.

b.

c.

What is the likely cause of the traits listed above?

CHAPTER TWO QUIZ

1. What happens when positive ions move into a neuron and negative ions move out? (2-3)

    a.   The cell goes into refraction
    b.   Transmitter substances are synthesized
    c.   The polarization of the cell increases
    d.   An action potential occurs

2. Chemicals released from nerve cells which play an important role in nerve cell communication are called (4)
    a.   neurovesicles
    b.   communication chemicals
    c.   transmission ions
    d.   neurotransmitters

3. Endorphins seem to be produced in response to (5)
    a.   pain
    b.   vigorous exercise
    c.   both pain and vigorous exercise
    d.   neither pain nor vigorous exercise

4. Using energy is to conserving energy as (6)
    a.   sympathetic is to parasympathetic
    b.   parasympathetic is to sympathetic
    c.   somatic is to autonomic
    d.   autonomic is to somatic

5. After being hit by a car, Elvis the dog's movements became jerky and not as coordinated. His owner attributes this change to brain damage in the _____ . (8)
    a.   thalamus
    b.   amygdala
    c.   cerebellum
    d.   temporal lobe

6. Vision is to audition as (10)
    a.   frontal lobe is to parietal lobe
    b.   parietal lobe is to frontal lobe
    c.   occipital lobe is to temporal lobe
    d.   temporal lobe is to occipital lobe

7. Research suggests that the left hemisphere of the brain in most people is dominant for: (12)

    a.   musical ability
    b.   creativity
    c.   perception of three-dimensional space
    d.   language ability

8.   The two hemispheres of the brain communicate with each other primarily through a wide band of nerve fibers that pass between them called the (13)
      a.   hemispheric channel
      b.   corpus callosum
      c.   tomographic connection
      d.   myelin sheath

9.   Which might be an outcome for a genetic male with adrenogenic insensitivity syndrome? (16)
      a.   born with distinctly female genitals
      b.   traditional female maternal interests
      c.   traditional female childhood play
      d.   all of the other alternatives are correct

10.   Traumatic brain injury refers to brain damage as a result of: (20)
      a.   drug induced neural damage
      b.   head injury from force applied to the skull
      c.   alcohol induced brain damage
      d.   all of the injuries listed in the other alternatives

CHAPTER 3

SENSATION AND PERCEPTION:
MAKING CONTACT WITH THE WORLD AROUND US

1. Define sensation and perception. Which of these two processes requires an active process by the organism? (90)

    a.   sensation

    b.   perception

    c.   active process

2. Define sensory receptors and give their location. (91)

    Define transduction.

3. Define absolute threshold and <u>describe why it fluctuates</u>. (92)

    Describe what signal detection theory suggests about absolute threshold. (92-93)

4. Wine tasters, fish inspectors, and auto mechanics are but three of the professions for which the difference threshold and the jnd are important. Define difference threshold and jnd and give an example of another profession which makes use of these concepts. (93)

    a.   difference threshold

b.   jnd

c.   profession

5.   Define subliminal perception and discuss the conclusions reached by your author concerning the possible effects of subliminal perception. (93-94)

a.   subliminal perception

b.   conclusion

6.   Define sensory adaptation. (94)

Describe how sensory adaptation can both help and/or hurt us. (95)

a.   help

b.   hurt

VISION

7.   Label the structures of the eye. (95-96)

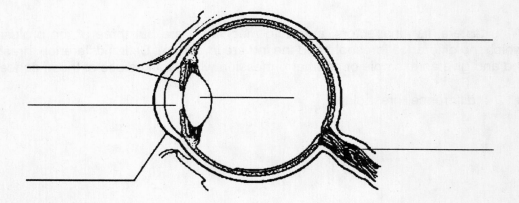

In the space below, draw your own cross-section of the eye, and label all the parts again.

Describe the following parts of the eye: (95-97, Use the running glossary on p. 95)

a.   cornea

b.   pupil

c.   iris

d.   lens

e.   retina

f.   cones

g.   rods

h.   fovea

i.   optic nerve

j.   blind spot

Using the above terms, write a paragraph describing the sequence of events as light energy is converted into signals our brain can understand. <u>Underline</u> the terms.

8.   Distinguish between rods and cones concerning: location in the retina, ability to see detail, ability to see color or black and white, and under which level of illumination each functions best. (95-97)

	location	detail	color or black and white	level of illumination
cones				
rods		poor detail	black and white	

9.   Describe the various aspects of visual activity listed below: (98-99)

a.   nearsightedness

b.   farsightedness

c.   dark adaptation

Describe saccadic movements and describe how they relate to reading.

10.   There are two theories of color vision. List and describe them. (99-100)

a.

b.

Describe the model of color vision most researchers now support. (100)

11.   Describe how our brain processes visual information. (101-102)

HEARING

12.   Describe sound localization and describe how it works. (106)

TOUCH AND OTHER SENSES

13.   List four skin senses. (107)

       a.

       b.

       c.

       d.

       What determines the skin's sensory experience. (107)

       Describe active touch and passive touch. Which is more accurate and why? (107)

       a.   active touch

       b.   passive touch

       c.   more accurate

14.   List and give an example of the two types of pain. (107-108)

a.

b.

Describe how the pain signal is transmitted. (107-108)

Describe how these two pain systems are used to explain the gate-control theory. (108-109)

Describe how these cognitive-behavioral procedures help with pain. (110)

SMELL AND TASTE: THE CHEMICAL SENSES

15.   Describe our ability to identify specific odors in terms of the number of molecules which must be present and the range of stimuli we can detect. (111)

Describe the effect of fragrances in the work place. (113)

KINESTHESIS AND VESTIBULAR SENSE

16.   Complete the following chart. (114)

SENSE	DEFINITION	LOCATION OF SENSORY ORGANS	KIND OF INFORMATION SENSE PROVIDES
Kinesthesia			
Vestibular Sense			

PERCEPTION: PUTTING IT ALL TOGETHER

Perception is the process through which we select, organize, and interpret the information from our sensory receptors -- the information of sensation.

17.   Describe selective attention and discuss the advantages and disadvantages it brings. (116)

Describe the cocktail party phenomenon. (Include features which attract our attention). (116)

18. Describe the innate tendencies of perceptual organization studied by Gestalt psychologists. (118-120)

	description	example
a.	figure-ground	
b.	law of similarity	
c.	law of proximity	
d.	law of good continuation	
e.	law of simplicity	
f.	law of common region	
g.	law of closure	

19.   Describe the important role that constancies play in our lives. (121-122)

       List and define the three constancies given in your text. (121)

       a.

       b.

       c.

20.   Describe how the theory of misapplied constancy is used to explain perceptual illusions. (122-123)

21.   We are able to perceive our visual world in three dimensions - including depth - because we make use of many cues. Define monocular and binocular cues. (126)

       List and describe the monocular cues and binocular cues we use. (126)

       <u>monocular cues</u>

       a.

       b.

       c.

       d.

       e.

f.

g.

binocular cues

a.

b.

EXTRASENSORY PERCEPTION: PERCEPTION WITHOUT SENSATION?

22.   Define Psi (or ESP). (129)

List and define four forms of ESP. (129)

a.

b.

c.

d.

Describe the three positions used to argue against the existence of ESP. (130)

a.

b.

c.

MAKING PSYCHOLOGY A PART OF YOUR LIFE

23.   Discuss the possible danger in using stereo headsets even at a seemingly low volume. (131)

CHAPTER THREE QUIZ

1.   The process of selecting, organizing and interpreting the input from sensory receptors is referred to as: (1)

    a.   convergence
    b.   transduction
    c.   sensation
    d.   perception

2.   You are inspecting an airplane and you think you hear a faint odd sound that can indicate that the plane should be grounded for repairs, but you aren't sure. If you ground the plane, the small company will be financially burdened; if you don't ground the plane and it was flawed, as many as 8 people could lose their lives. Your approach to making the decision is an example of: (3)

    a.   signal detection theory
    b.   gate-control theory
    c.   frequency theory
    d.   vergence movements theory

3.   Dark adaptation results in: (9)

    a.   decreased sensitivity to light
    b.   increased sensitivity to light
    c.   increased abilities to perceive hues
    d.   decreased abilities to perceive feature detectors

4.   Which of the following theories suggests that color vision can be explained on the basis of unique receptors sensitive to red, green, or blue? (10)

    a.   opponent process
    b.   trichromatic
    c.   signal detection
    d.   gate-control

5.   Which of the following theories suggests that there are neural mechanisms in the spinal cord that sometimes close, thus preventing pain messages from reaching the brain? (14)

    a.   pain inhibition theory
    b.   Substance P theory
    c.   gate-control theory
    d.   signal detection theory

6.   A pleasant fragrance in the work environment: (15)

    a.   increases worker self confidence
    b.   increases willingness to compromise among workers
    c.   improves performance
    d.   all of the other alternatives are correct

7.   Your ability to detect that your arm is moving when in a darkened room is due to: (16)

    a.   the haptic sense
    b.   kinesthesia
    c.   the vestibular sense
    d.   none of the items listed in the other alternatives

8.   The "cocktail party phenomenon" is an example of: (17)

    a.   selective attention
    b.   prosopagnosia
    c.   prototypical attention
    d.   unconscious processing

9.   If one object partially obscures another object in a painting, the artist has used _____ as a cue to the relative distance of the objects from the viewer. (21)

    a.   interposition
    b.   convergence
    c.   linear perspective
    d.   accommodation

10.   The ability to affect the physical world purely by thoughts is called: (22)

    a.   precognition
    b.   telepathy
    c.   clairvoyance
    d.   psychokinesis

CHAPTER 4

CONSCIOUSNESS:
AWARENESS OF OURSELVES AND THE EXTERNAL WORLD

1.   Define states of consciousness. (136)

BIOLOGICAL RHYTHMS:
TIDES OF LIFE AND CONSCIOUS EXPERIENCE

2.   Describe circadian rhythms. (136-137)

      Give examples of two other biological rhythms which are not circadian. Indicate how
      long the cycle is in each case. (137)

      Describe four differences in circadian rhythms between "larks" and "owls". (139-140)

      a.

      b.

      c.

      d.

3.   Describe how the suprachiasmatic nucleus, pineal gland, and melatonin are involved
      in the regulation of circadian rhythms. (138)

Define seasonal affective disorder (SAD). (138)

Describe how SAD can be related to the biological structures described above. (138-139)

4.   Describe how circadian rhythms influence the experience of jet lag. (140)

How does shift work affect circadian rhythms? (140)

What basic knowledge about the nature of circadian rhythms should employers utilize in planning shift schedules? (141)

a.

b.

WAKING STATES OF CONSCIOUSNESS: EVERYDAY EXPERIENCES

5.   There appear to be two different ways of controlling ongoing activities - two levels of attention to, or conscious control over, our behavior. Contrast automatic and controlled processing. (142)

6.   Define daydreams. (143)

Distinguish between daydreams and hallucinations. (143-144)

Describe four useful functions which daydreams may serve. (144)

a.

b.

c.

d.

7.   When we focus our attention on ourselves, we enter a state of self-consciousness. Distinguish between private and public self-consciousness. (145)

Describe one example of the effects of self-consciousness, the choking under pressure effect. (146)

Use the principle of the choking under pressure concept to explain why an opposing team might call a time-out just before a kicker attempts a possible game-winning field goal. (146)

SLEEP: THE PAUSE THAT REFRESHES

8.   Define sleep. (147)

Define the following terms, which are related to the study of sleep. (147-149)

a.   electroencephalogram (EEG)

b.   rapid eye movement (REM) sleep

Describe the state of consciousness associated with each of the following: (148)

a.   beta brain waves

b.   alpha brain waves

c.   delta brain wave

Complete the following statements: (148-149)

There are _____ stages of sleep. During rapid eye movement (REM) sleep, there is an almost total _____ of activity in body muscles. Periods of REM sleep continue to _____ with other stages of sleep throughout the night, and _____ in length towards the morning.

9.   Most sleep researchers believe that sleep serves a restorative function, a circadian function, or some combination of the two. Describe the restorative theory regarding the function of sleep. (149)

Is there much direct evidence for this theory? (149)

What are the effects upon task performance, mood, health, and sleep patterns for volunteers who have reduced their nightly sleep to five hours or less? (150)

a.   task performance

b.   mood

c.   health

d.   sleep patterns

A second theory on the function of sleep emphasizes the relationship of sleep to basic circadian rhythms. Describe this theory as it applies to the purpose of sleep. (150)

Describe the relationship between sleep and our waking moods. (151)

10.   List five tactics that might be helpful when you are having difficult falling asleep. (152)

   a.

   b.

   c.

   d.

   e.

   Define the following sleep disorders: (152-153)

   a.   insomnia

   b.   somnambulism

   c.   night terrors

   d.   nightmares

   e.   nocturnal myoclonus

   f.   hypersomnias

   g.   narcolepsy

11.   Briefly answer the following questions. (153-154)

   a.   Does everybody dream?

   b.   How long do dreams last?

c.   Can external events be incorporated into dreams?

d.   If a man experiences an erection or a woman experiences vaginal secretions during sleep, does this mean the sleeper is having a sexy dream?

e.   Do dreams really express unconscious wishes?

f.   When people cannot recall their dreams, does this mean that they are purposely forgetting them, perhaps because they find the content of their dreams too disturbing?

12.   Describe Freud's theory concerning the purpose of dreams. Include in your description the distinction between the latent and the manifest content of dreams. (155)

What do psychologists currently believe about Freud's views concerning the purpose of dreams? (155)

What does cross-cultural research indicate with respect to Freud's theory of dreams? (155-156)

13.   There are theories about dreams other than Freud's. Describe the following theories about dreaming. (156-158)

a.   The physiological theory

b.   The cognitive view (see figure 4.4)

HYPNOSIS:
ALTERED STATE OF CONSCIOUSNESS OR SOCIAL ROLE PLAYING

14.   Define hypnosis. (158)

        List the five characteristics of individuals who are most susceptible to hypnosis. (159)

        a.

        b.

        c.

        d.

        e.

        What conclusions seem justified concerning the effects of hypnosis? (161)

CONSCIOUSNESS-ALTERING DRUGS:
WHAT THEY ARE AND WHAT THEY DO

15.   Define consciousness-altering drugs. (163)

Describe what is meant by drug abuse. (163)

Define the following terms, important in understanding drug abuse. (163)

a.   physiological dependence

b.   psychological dependence

c.   tolerance

d.   cross-tolerance

16.   Describe the learning perspective concerning why drug abuse occurs. (163-164)

Describe the psychodynamic perspective concerning drug abuse. (164)

Describe the social perspective concerning drug abuse. (164)

Describe the cognitive perspective (Tiffany's automatic processing theory) concerning drug abuse. (164-165, see Key Points, 164)

17.   If consciousness-altering drugs are categorized by their psychological effects, they can be placed into four categories. Below you will find the four categories along with some specific drugs listed under each category. Describe the categories and the potential harmful physiological and psychological effects of the listed drugs. (165-168; and see 169)

   a.   depressants

        1)   alcohol

        2)   barbiturates

   b.   stimulants

        1)   cocaine

   c.   opiates

        1)   heroin

   d.   psychedelics and hallucinogens

        1)   marijuana

        2)   LSD

18.   List and describe four factors which can change the effects of consciousness-altering
       drugs. (168-170)

   a.

   b.

   c.

   d.

PSYCHOLOGY: PART OF YOUR LIFE

19.   List three psychological benefits that you may expect to obtain from meditating. (171)

     a.

     b.

     c.

CHAPTER FOUR QUIZ

1. Which of the following is an example of a circadian rhythm? (2)

    a. dreaming
    b. hunger
    c. menstruation
    d. sleeping

2. Harvey dislikes the cold and snow and spends most of the Minnesota winters indoors reading and watching television. If Harvey is predisposed to a seasonal affective disorder, during the winter he is likely to experience: (3)

    a. sleepiness and fatigue
    b. an increase in melatonin secretion
    c. depression
    d. all of the alternatives are correct

3. Henrik has been typing for so many years now that he finds he can transcribe handwritten material almost mindlessly. Henrik is apparently using _____ processing when he types. (5)

    a. controlled
    b. automatic
    c. focused
    d. high-flexibility

4. An awareness of how we appear to other persons is referred to as _____ self-consciousness. (7)

    a. public
    b. internal
    c. private
    d. external

5. In her first big tennis tournament, Martina choked under pressure. She did much worse than she had in her practices. This performance decline can be attributed to: (7)

    a. increased self-consciousness interfering with automatic control of behaviors
    b. playing in an automatic fashion, rather than paying close attention to the components of the game
    c. underuse of control processing and overuse of automatic processing
    d. the higher quality of her opponents

6. The brain waves exhibited during the deepest level of sleep (stage four) were _____ brain waves. (8)

    a. beta
    b. alpha
    c. theta
    d. delta

7.   Freud referred to the hidden meaning of dreams as the _____ content of
      dreams. (12)

      a.   manifest
      b.   unrevealed
      c.   latent
      d.   mysterious

8.   Katrina is likely to have high hypnotic susceptibility since she: (14)

      a.   has a low IQ
      b.   often daydreams in vivid visual imagery
      c.   often suffers from insomnia
      d.   practices meditation

9.   Which perspective believes that drug abuse occurs because it is the "in" thing to do
      and because of peer pressure? (16)

      a.   The learning perspective
      b.   The psychodynamic perspective
      c.   The social perspective
      d.   The cognitive perspective

10.   _____ reduce activity in the nervous system, produce lethargy, and
      cause a pronounced slowing of almost all bodily functions. (17)

      a.   hallucinogens
      b.   stimulants
      c.   opiates
      d.   paradoxical drugs

CHAPTER 5

LEARNING:
HOW WE'RE CHANGED BY EXPERIENCE

NOTE: Conditioning is a term psychologists use to refer to learning. You may find it helpful to substitute the word learned for conditioned.

1.   Define learning. (176)

CLASSICAL CONDITIONING:
LEARNING THAT SOME STIMULI SIGNAL OTHERS

2.   List the three forms of conditioning, and briefly describe each type. (176)

    a.

    b.

    c.

    List four examples of reactions learned as a result of classical conditioning. (177)

    a.

    b.

    c.

    d.

3.   Describe the sequence of events leading to classical conditioning. Use the terms neutral stimulus (NS), unconditioned stimulus (UCS), unconditioned response (UCR), conditioned stimulus (CS), and conditioned response (CR). (177-181 and see Figs 5.1 and 5.4)

NOTE: Conditioning occurs as a result of the pairing of the CS and UCS.

4.   Identify extinction, reconditioning, and spontaneous recovery from the definitions below. (181-182)

   a.   _____ Following extinction, and after a rest period, the recurrence of a conditioned response without additional pairing of the CS-UCS.

   b.   _____ The gradual disappearance of a conditioned response because of the repeated presentation of the conditioned stimulus without the unconditioned stimulus.

   c.   _____ Following extinction, the rapid recovery of a conditioned response upon reinstatement of a CS-UCS pairing.

5.   Explain the difference between stimulus generalization and stimulus discrimination. (182-183)

   Pretend that you are a child and a large black dog jumped on you and growled angrily. Use this situation to give examples of stimulus generalization and stimulus discrimination.

   a.   stimulus generalization

   b.   stimulus discrimination

6.   Describe the conclusion which can be drawn from the Garcia and Koelling (1966) research on rats and saccharin-flavored water as well as similar findings from other studies. (183-184)

   Define conditioned taste aversion. (184-185)

   Give an example of food you were conditioned to avoid which resulted from conditioned taste aversion.

7.   Cognition refers to mental processes such as thinking. Describe the research (Rescorla & Wagner, 1972) which suggests a cognitive component in classical conditioning. (186)

8.   List and describe two classically conditioned procedures for reducing anxiety to stimuli. (187-188)

      a.

      b.

OPERANT CONDITIONING:
LEARNING BASED ON CONSEQUENCES

9.   All reinforcements increase or strengthen behavioral responses. List and describe two types of reinforcements. (190-191) Do not use the definition on page 190.

      a.

      b.

NOTE: Negative **and** positive reinforcements strengthen behavioral responses. In a negative reinforcement situation, the organism is in an aversive (or potentially aversive) situation, which ends as soon as the behavior is performed, thus strengthening the behavior. (see Key Concept on page 192)

List and describe the two procedures which weaken behavioral responses. (191)

      a.

      b.

10.   Demonstrate your understanding of the Premack Principle by describing an example of this principle not found in your text. (190)

11.   Describe the difference between punishment and negative reinforcement. Be sure to include what happens to the frequency of the behavior when each is administered. (192)

       a.

       b.

12.   From the list of words which follows, fill in the blanks: **voluntary, B. F. Skinner, consequences, elicited, Ivan Pavlov, unconditioned, emitted**. (186, 193)

       In classical conditioning, behaviors are learned through the process of association, i.e. associating a conditioned stimulus (CS) with a(n) _____ stimulus. In operant conditioning, learning involves the relationship between behaviors and their _____. Classically conditioned behaviors are reflexes (involuntary), and can be _____. Operant behaviors on the other hand are _____ and are _____. An important theorist in classical conditioning was _____ _____, and in operant conditioning an important theorist was _____ _____ _____, who also designed the _____ box.

13.   Describe shaping and chaining, and describe how each is conditioned. (193-195)

       a.

       b.

       Make up your own example of shaping and chaining.

       a.   shaping

       b.   chaining

14.   State which type of reinforcement schedule is more powerful in maintaining conditioned behavior. (196)

Schedules of reinforcement are rules for determining when and how reinforcements will be delivered. List, define, and give examples of the five schedules of reinforcement. Underline what must happen before reinforcement is available in each schedule. (196-197)

a.

example

b.

example

c.

example

d.

example

e.

example

15.   Define discriminative stimulus. (198) (see glossary)

List three discriminative stimuli which trigger your eating behavior.

a.

b.

c.

16.   Describe how learned helplessness is acquired. (200-202)

Describe what happens when the situation changes.

Explain how learned helplessness is related to cognitive processes. (200)

OBSERVATIONAL LEARNING:
LEARNING FROM THE BEHAVIOR AND OUTCOMES OF OTHERS

17.   List and describe the four factors that Bandura identified as important in observational learning. (206-208, see fig 5.11)

a.

b.

c.

d.

Explain the role observation learning plays in aggressive behavior. (208-209)

Explain how observational learning might be used to train workers to interact more effectively with people from different cultural backgrounds. (210)

18.   Complete the following chart.

	CLASSICAL CONDITIONING 176-188 212	OPERANT CONDITIONING 189-206 212-213	OBSERVATIONAL LEARNING 206-211 213
Describe how Conditioning Occurs			
Note the following terms which are associated with each type of conditioning	learning UCS, UCR, CS, CR extinction reconditioning spontaneous recovery stimulus generalization stimulus discrimination conditioned taste aversion	reinforcement positive reinforcers negative reinforcers Premack principle punishment omission training shaping discriminative stimulus	observational learning models
Names of Major Theorists associated with these three types of conditioning			

CHAPTER FIVE QUIZ

1.　　Learning is defined as: (1)

    a.　　changes in behavior due to maturation
    b.　　new behaviors that develop over time
    c.　　changes in behavior resulting from experience
    d.　　the development of problem-solving ability

2.　　The salivation that would be produced by meat powder would be termed a(n): (3)

    a.　　learned response
    b.　　reinforcer
    c.　　conditioned response
    d.　　unconditioned response

3.　　When the unconditioned stimulus no longer follows the conditioned stimulus, _____ occurs. (4)

    a.　　recovery
    b.　　extinction
    c.　　induction
    d.　　frustration

4.　　The process by which organisms learn to respond to certain stimuli and to not respond to others is called: (5)

    a.　　stimulus generalization
    b.　　flooding
    c.　　punishment
    d.　　stimulus discrimination

5.　　Some alcoholics are given a drug called Antabuse which reacts with alcohol to cause nausea and vomiting. The use of Antabuse to treat alcoholism is an application of (6)

    a.　　higher-order conditioning
    b.　　negative reinforcement
    c.　　conditioned taste aversion
    d.　　stimulus generalization

6.   Which of the following is an example of flooding? (8)

a.   Mia is allergic to peanuts and soon develops an aversion to peanut butter and peanut candy.
b.   Darrell's mother used to bake homemade bread and now whenever Darrell walks past a bakery, the smell reminds him of home.
c.   Lucy, who suffers from the eating disorder of anorexia nervosa, feels stomach pains after any meal, and then avoids the type of food she has just consumed.
d.   Anne has been afraid of dogs since she was a child, so she spends lots of time with friends' dogs in order to get used to them and get over her fear.

7.   If Homer cleans up the barn, Pa gives him a five dollar bill. The five dollar bill is a _____ reinforcer. (9)

a.   partial reinforcer
b.   positive reinforcer
c.   negative reinforcer
d.   primary reinforcer

8.   In classical conditioning, the behavior is _____, whereas in operant conditioning, behavior is _____. (12)

a.   voluntary/involuntary
b.   elicited/emitted
c.   emitted/elicited
d.   changed/maintained

9.   A factory worker receives a pay check every two weeks. This is an example of (14)

a.   fixed-interval reinforcement
b.   fixed-ratio reinforcement
c.   variable-interval reinforcement
d.   variable-ratio reinforcement

10.   A farmer finds that no matter what he does, his crops seem to fall victim to the weather. If his crops continue to fail, the farmer may develop: (16)

a.   spontaneous recovery
b.   vicarious reinforcement
c.   aggravated depression
d.   learned helplessness

CHAPTER 6

MEMORY:
OF THINGS REMEMBERED . . . AND FORGOTTEN

HUMAN MEMORY: THE INFORMATION PROCESSING APPROACH

1.   Human memory has been described as similar but not identical to computer memory. Name and describe the three tasks common to both memory systems. (217)

        a.

        b.

        c.

2.   Name and describe each of our three distinct memory systems. Include in your descriptions both the duration and capacity of each system. (217-218 and see Fig. 6.1)

        a.

        b.

        c.

        Describe the way that information moves from sensory to short-term memory, and from short-term to long-term memory. (218 and see Fig. 6.1)

        a.   sensory to short-term memory

b.   short-term to long term memory

3.   According to the parallel distributed processing model, information is not processed step by-step, but simultaneously in several different parts of our total memory system. Describe how these several different parts operate. (218)

Why do many psychologists find this model so appealing? (218-219)

4.   Psychologists have concluded that most information in memory falls into one of three types of memory. List, describe, and give an example of each of the three types of memory. (220)

a.

b.

c.

SENSORY MEMORY: GATEWAY TO CONSCIOUSNESS

5.   Explain the function of sensory memory. (221 and see Figure 6.1)

Describe the following two characteristics of sensory memory: (Figure 6.1)

a.   capacity

b.   duration

Describe two conclusions found in Sperling's studies and confirmed in many later studies. (221-222)

a.

b.

SHORT-TERM MEMORY: THE WORKBENCH OF CONSCIOUSNESS

6.   Describe some scientific evidence for the existence of short term memory and the view that it is different from long term memory.

   a.   serial position curve (222 and see Figure 6.2)

   b.   word length effect (222-223)

   c.   acoustic coding (223)

   d.   semantic coding (223)

7.   List and describe the two ways in which information is represented in short-term memory. (224)

   a.

   b.

   How many pieces of information can be held in short-term memory? (224)

   Describe how the units of information called chunks allow us to store an increased amount of information in short-term memory. (224)

How long does information in short-term memory last? (224)

Describe how information can be kept in short-term memory for a longer period of time. (224)

LONG-TERM MEMORY: THE STOREHOUSE OF CONSCIOUSNESS

8.   Define long-term memory. (224-225)

Define the tip-of-the-tongue phenomenon. (225)

Describe what is indicated by the existence of the tip-of-the-tongue phenomenon. (225)

9.   Describe how information enters long-term memory from short-term memory. (225)

Explain how the levels of processing view relates to the amount of information retained in long term memory. Include and underline the terms shallow processing and deep processing in your explanation. (226-227)

10.   Define retrieval. (227)

Define storage. (228)

Describe how organization of materials is related to retrieval and storage. (228)

11.   Define and give an example of a retrieval cue. (228)

List, describe, and give examples of two kinds of retrieval cues. (228-229)

a.

b.

FORGETTING FROM LONG-TERM MEMORY

12.   Describe the trace decay hypothesis concerning why we forget material stored in long-term memory. (230)

Describe the interference perspective of forgetting. Include in your description the terms retroactive and proactive interference. (231 and Figure 6.6)

Give an example of retroactive interference. (231)

Give an example of proactive interference. (231)

13.   Define repression as a third cause of forgetting from long term memory. (232)

The concept of repression is generally accepted by health care professionals as well as by society as a whole. However, there are some instances of repressed memories of childhood sexual abuse that may not be accurate. Describe three reasons Loftus gives for regarding some of these claims with a healthy degree of skepticism. (232-233)

a.

b.

c.

14.   Define prospective memory. (233)

Describe two factors involved in prospective forgetting. (234)

    a.

    b.

MEMORY IN NATURAL CONTEXTS

15.   Describe the most likely reason for infantile amnesia, the inability to remember autobiographical events that occur before the age of two or three. (237-238)

16.   Define flashbulb memories. (239)

    Give an example of a flashbulb memory in your own life.

    Are flashbulb memories always accurate?

17.   List and describe two basic types of errors that frequently affect memory in natural contexts. (240)

    a.

    b.

Define schemas and describe the role they play with respect to encoding. Include in your description the difference between the effects of new and old schemas. (240-241)

Since schemas develop out of experience, it seems reasonable to assume that people raised in different cultures would develop schemas that reflect these differences and would be more likely to notice and remember information consistent with those schemas. Discuss the results of Pritchard's (1991) comparison of high school students in the U.S. and Palau. (242 and see Figure 6.9)

Describe one possible reason for the occurrence of memory construction, our tendency to fill in details or even to remember experiences we never had when recalling past events. (243)

18.   Describe the three interviewing procedures that increased witnesses' accuracy by almost fifty percent. (244)

        a.

        b.

        c.

Summarize the research and state your author's conclusion regarding the use of hypnosis as a technique for improving eyewitness memory. (245)

Discuss the effect of alcohol on eyewitness memory. (245)

THE BIOLOGICAL BASES OF MEMORY: HOW THE BRAIN STORES KNOWLEDGE

19. List and describe two kinds of amnesias or memory disorders. (246)

a.

b.

Describe the amnesia suffered in the earlier and later stages of Alzheimer's Disease. (249)

a. earlier stages

b. later stages

20. Describe where the brain stores specific memories. (249-250)

Describe how the information is actually stored.

MAKING PSYCHOLOGY PART OF YOUR LIFE

21.   List and describe six suggestions for increasing our ability to remember more
       information with greater accuracy. (250-251)

       a.

       b.

       c.

       d.

       e.

       f.

CHAPTER SIX QUIZ

1.   The way information is entered into memory is called: (1)

     a.   retrieval
     b.   encoding
     c.   storage
     d.   programming

2.   Information goes from sensory memory to short-term memory when we: (2)

     a.   attend to it
     b.   rehearse it
     c.   ignore it
     d.   retrieve it

3.   Memory for specific times or places is called: (4)

     a.   episodic
     b.   semantic
     c.   univariate
     d.   associationistic

4.   The first memory structure involved in the encoding of information is: (5)

     a.   sensory memory
     b.   short-term memory
     c.   long-term memory
     d.   procedural memory

5.   Short-term memory can hold _____ separate items. (7)

     a.   2 to 3
     b.   4 to 5
     c.   7 to 9
     d.   8 to 10

6.   Research on the levels of processing indicates that memory is better with _____ processing. (9)

     a.   deep
     b.   shallow
     c.   moderate
     d.   rote

7.   Stimuli that are associated with information stored in memory and aid in retrieval are called _____. (11)

     a.   loci
     b.   state-dependent
     c.   cues
     d.   phonological loops

8.   When items learned now interfere with those learned earlier, the interference is called: (12)

     a.   reactive
     b.   retroactive
     c.   proactive
     d.   anticipatory

9.   Our memory for things we are supposed to do in the future is called: (14)

     a.   retrospective memory
     b.   futuristic memory
     c.   procedural memory
     d.   prospective memory

10. When we fill in details of events to make memories more complete, we are using: (17)

     a.   association
     b.   shallow processing
     c.   construction
     d.   distortion

CHAPTER 7

COGNITION:
THINKING, DECIDING, COMMUNICATING

THINKING: FORMING CONCEPTS AND REASONING TO CONCLUSIONS

1. Describe the two main strategies adopted by psychologists to try to understand the pattern of consciousness. (256)

    a.

    b.

2. Describe two theories of how concepts are represented in consciousness. (258-259)

    a.

    b.

3. Schemas and concepts are closely related. Describe how they are similar and how they are different. (259)

    a.   similar

    b.   different

4.   A proposition is a sentence that relates one concept to another, or one feature of the concept to the entire concept. Give two examples (not already included in your text) of propositions. (259)

   a.

   b.

5.   Research findings suggest that once we form a mental image we think about it by scanning visually, just as we would if it actually existed. Describe two studies that support this theory. (259-260 and see Figure 7.1)

   a.   Kosslyn, 1980

   b.   Baum & Jonides, 1979

6.   Other research suggests that visual images are actually embedded in our knowledge rather than simply scanned. Describe a study that supports this view. (260)

7.   Describe the difference between formal reasoning and everyday reasoning. (260-261)

8.   Describe four factors that, working together, seem to reduce our ability to reason effectively. (262-264)

    a.

    b.

    c.

    d.

9.   Describe the ecological approach to animal cognition and include how it differs from earlier approaches. (265)

MAKING DECISIONS: CHOOSING AMONG ALTERNATIVES

10.   List the two factors that a perfectly rational decision maker would consider. (257)

a.

b.

11.   Define heuristics. (267)

List and describe three heuristics that tend to be used most frequently. (267-269)

a.

b.

c.

12.   Describe how framing a situation can affect the decision-making process. (269-270)

13.   Define and give an example of escalation of commitment. (271)

14.   Describe several different factors that Straw and Ross (1987) have suggested as
       possible causes of escalation of commitment. (271-272 and see Figure 7.5)

       Describe three techniques that can be used to counter escalation. (273)

       a.

       b.

       c.

PROBLEM SOLVING AND CREATIVITY: FINDING PATHS TO DESIRED GOALS

15. Describe four major aspects of problem solving. (274-275 and see Figure 7.6)

     a.

     b.

     c.

     d.

16. Contrast the problem-solving strategies of American and Chinese children. (275-276)

     What do these results suggest?

17. List and describe two subtle factors that interfere with effective problem solving. (277-278)

     a.

     b.

18.   Define creativity. (279)

Psychologists who have studied creativity find that it is not likely to spring up suddenly from flashes of inspiration but rather to involve a series of specific steps. Describe the four steps discussed in your text. (279)

a.

b.

c.

d.

Define divergent thinking. (279)

Define convergent thinking. (279)

Which of these two types of thinking, convergent or divergent thinking is associated with creativity? (279)

List and describe five steps individuals and society can use to foster creativity. (280)

a.

b.

c.

d.

e.

19.   Define artificial intelligence. (281)

LANGUAGE: THE COMMUNICATION OF INFORMATION

20.   Most scientists agree that what truly sets humans apart from other species is the use of language. Define language. (282)

List three criteria that must be met in order for a set of symbols to be viewed as language. (282-283)

a.

b.

c.

List the two major components involved in the actual use of language. (283)

a.

b.

21.　　Describe the difference between surface structure and deep structure, including in your description a definition of both terms. (283-284)

Describe Noam Chomsky's theory of how language is understood. (283-284)

22.　　Describe the cognitive theory of language development. (284-285)

23.   List and describe the three components of language development. (285)

a.

b.

c.

Define the following terms that relate to the steps in a child's language development: (285-287)

a.   babbling

b.   phonological strategies

c.   object words

d.   action words

e.   holophrases

f.   telegraphic speech

24.   Describe the psychologists' conclusions regarding the ability of animals to use language. (290)

Describe the other side of the argument. (290)

MAKING PSYCHOLOGY PART OF YOUR LIFE

25.   List four guidelines for making good decisions. (291)

   a.

   b.

   c.

   d.

CHAPTER SEVEN QUIZ

1.   Concepts can be represented as: (2)

    a.   images
    b.   features
    c.   schemas
    d.   all of the above

2.   Thoughts are organized into _____ which group or classify objects, events, or ideas. (3)

    a.   premises
    b.   rules
    c.   concepts
    d.   images

3.   Failing to see faults in your physician's diagnosis of your health problem might best be explained as an example of (8)

    a.   divergent thinking
    b.   formal reasoning
    c.   syllogisms
    d.   oversight bias

4.   Recent research suggests that (9)

    a.   only humans use cognitive processes
    b.   humans and other animals use syllogisms
    c.   humans and many other animals use cognitive processes
    d.   without language cognitive processes can not be used

5.   According to the availability heuristic, the more easily we think of something, the more _____. (11)

    a.   frequently, we judge it to be
    b.   we like it
    c.   we dislike it
    d.   we understand it

6.   External factors stemming from group pressures begin to play a role in the escalation of commitment process: (14)

    a.   during its initial phase
    b.   when there are early losses
    c.   when there are continuing losses
    d.   during all of its phases

7.   The style of thinking most likely to produce creative outcomes is known as
        _____. (18)

        a.   expert thinking
        b.   novice thinking
        c.   convergent thinking
        d.   divergent thinking

8.   According to Chomsky, the underlying meaning contained in a sentence is known as:
        (21)

        a.   phoneme
        b.   morpheme
        c.   deep structure
        d.   surface structure

9.   What are the three basic components of language development? (23)

        a.   overextension, underextension, operating principles
        b.   phonological, semantic, grammatical
        c.   intuitive, semantic, phonological
        d.   deep structure, surface structure, fast mapping

10.   Which of the following is not part of your textbook's advice for making good
        decisions? (25)

        a.   Trust your memory.
        b.   Question all anchors.
        c.   Remain flexible.
        d.   Consider all options.

CHAPTER 8

HUMAN DEVELOPMENT I:
THE CHILDHOOD YEARS

PHYSICAL GROWTH AND DEVELOPMENT

1. Developmental psychologists study three major categories of change. Describe each of these major categories. (296)

    a. Physical growth and development

    b. Cognitive development

    c. Social-emotional development

2. There are three stages of prenatal development. Describe development during: (297)

    a. The period of the ovum (after fertilization)

    b. The period of the embryo

    c. The period of the fetus

3. Many environmental factors known as teratogens can damage the developing fetus. List and briefly describe the influence of each of the following teratogens. (298-299)

    a. Disease during pregnancy

b.   Prescription and over-the-counter drugs

c.   The Fetal Alcohol Syndrome

d.   Smoking

4.   Describe physical development during the first year of infancy in terms of body weight and height. (299)

a.   weight

b.   height

List five simple reflexes that are present at birth. (299)

a.

b.

c.

d.

e.

5.   Studies have demonstrated that newborns have the ability to learn. Describe the conditions under which newborns can be classically conditioned. (299-300)

Describe the evidence which shows that newborn babies can be operantly conditioned. (300)

Describe the evidence which shows that newborn babies can learn through imitation. (301)

6.   Ingenious methods of research have revealed that newborns and infants are capable of perceiving many aspects of the physical world - more aspects than were formerly assumed. Describe the perceptual world of the infant in terms of the following categories: (301-302)

a.   colors

b.   sounds

c.   tastes

d.   form/pattern perception

Describe the visual cliff apparatus and what it is used to test. (302)

According to research, when does depth perception first appear?

7.   Developmental psychologists use different research methods for studying human development. Describe the following research methods and discuss the strengths and weaknesses of each: (302-304; and see Figure 8.2)

a.   Longitudinal Research

1)   strengths

a)

b)

    2)   weaknesses

            a)

            b)

   b.   Cross-sectional Research

    1)   strengths

            a)

            b)

    2)   weakness

            a)

   c.   Longitudinal-Sequential Design

    1)   strengths

            a)

            b)

    2)   weaknesses (potential)

            a)

            b)

COGNITIVE DEVELOPMENT: CHANGES IN HOW WE KNOW THE EXTERNAL WORLD...AND OURSELVES

8.   According to Piaget, adaptation is the mechanism that underlies cognitive development. Define adaptation and its two basic components: assimilation and accommodation. (305)

   a.   Adaptation

    1)   assimilation

    2)   accommodation

9.   Piaget proposed a stage theory of cognitive development. Describe cognitive
      development during each of the stages of Piaget's theory. (305-307)

      a.   Sensorimotor Stage

      b.   Preoperational Stage

      c.   Concrete Operations

      d.   Formal Operations

      Define the following terms discussed in Piaget's theory of cognitive development. For
      each term, also list the stage when it appears. (305-307).

      a.   object permanence

      b.   make-believe play

      c.   egocentrism

      d.   conservation

      e.   hypothetico-deductive reasoning

      f.   propositional reasoning

10.   There have been a number of criticisms of Piaget's theory of cognitive development.
      Describe the general agreement among developmental psychologists regarding the
      inaccuracies of Piaget's theory. (309)

11.   During the past twenty years an alternative approach to understanding cognitive development has emerged and has gained support among psychologists. This approach is known as the information processing approach. Psychologists who adopt this approach seek to understand how children's capacities to process, store, retrieve, and actively manipulate information increase with age.

Describe the findings of the study/investigation that demonstrated that newborns can readily form mental representations of stimuli to which they are exposed. (310)

Describe how younger and older children differ with respect to attentional focus and planfulness. (310)

a.   younger children

b.   older children

Define attention-deficit hyperactivity disorder. (311)

Describe how children's short-term and long-term memory improves with age. (311-312)

a.   short-term memory

b.   long-term memory

Define script. (312)

Give an example of a script from your own childhood experiences.

Describe metacognition. (312)

12.   According to Kohlberg, there are three distinct levels of moral development and six stages of moral understanding. Describe the three levels of moral development. (315-317; also see Table 8.1)

a.   Preconventional Level

   b.   Conventional Level

   c.   Postconventional Level

   Describe how Kohlberg measured moral reasoning. (315)

   Is moral development universal or culture related? (317-318)

13.   Gilligan suggests that Kohlberg's theory of moral development is sex-biased. Describe
      an important benefit of Gilligan's research on moral development. (319)

SOCIAL AND EMOTIONAL DEVELOPMENT:
FORMING RELATIONSHIPS WITH OTHERS

14.   Define social referencing. (320)

15.   Define temperament. (320)

16.   Chess and Thomas (1977) were able to classify infants according to their
      temperaments. Describe three temperamental characteristics identified below and give
      the percentage of children in each classification. (321)

   a.   Easy children

   b.   Difficult children

   c.   Slow-to-Warm-Up Children

17.   Summarize the findings of studies on the stability of infant temperament. (321-322)

18.   Define attachment. (322)

Describe how the strange situation test assesses the strength of attachment. (322-323)

Describe the behavior of securely attached, avoidantly attached, resistantly attached, and disorganized attached infants and give the percentage of children identified in each classification. (323)

a.   securely attached

b.   avoidantly attached

c.   resistantly attached

d.   disorganized attached

Describe the two factors that determine the pattern of attachment shown by a child. (324)

a.

b.

Is day care a threat to secure attachment? (325)

19.   Describe the conclusions of Harlow's research regarding contact comfort and attachment among baby rhesus monkeys. (325-326)

Do such effects occur among human babies as well?

20.   Contrast the roles that mothers and fathers play in the attachment process (326)

a.   mother's role

b.   father's role

GENDER: THE DEVELOPMENT OF GENDER IDENTITY AND SEX-STEREOTYPES BEHAVIOR

21.   Define gender identity. (327)

        Briefly describe the following two views of how gender identity is acquired. (327)

        a.   social learning theory

                1)   observational learning

                2)   operant conditioning

        b.   gender schema theory

22.   Define sex-role stereotypes. (328)

        Define sex-stereotyped behaviors. (328)

        Describe the two ways in which sex stereotyped beliefs and behaviors are acquired. (329-330)

        a.

        b.

MAKING PSYCHOLOGY A PART OF YOUR LIFE

23.   List six basic principles of successful parenthood. (331)

        a.

        b.

        c.

        d.

        e.

        f.

CHAPTER EIGHT QUIZ

1. Three major categories considered when examining shifts due to age include: (1)

   a. physical growth, assimilation, and attachment
   b. cognitive development, social and emotional development, and attachment
   c. physical growth, cognitive development, and accommodation
   d. physical growth, cognitive development, and social and emotional development

2. About two weeks after fertilization the fertilized ovum becomes implanted in the wall of the uterus. This marks the beginning of the _____ period of prenatal development: (2)

   a. placenta
   b. fetal
   c. embryonic
   d. zygotic

3. Disease during pregnancy, such as AIDS, over-the-counter drugs, such as aspirin, and alcohol are all examples of: (3)

   a. pathos substances
   b. analgesics
   c. teratogens
   d. neural inhibitors

4. Which of the following is **not** a reflex that is present at birth?: (4)

   a. sucking
   b. crawling
   c. following a moving light with eyes
   d. grasping

5. Research with the visual cliff apparatus suggests that depth perception is developed in humans as early as: (6)

   a. six days
   b. six months (when infants start to crawl)
   c. one year (when infants start to walk)
   d. birth

6. A research technique in which the same individuals are studied over substantial periods of time is called: (7)

   a. cross-sectional method
   b. age-similarity method
   c. longitudinal method
   d. age-transfer method

7.   According to Piaget, the process of understanding the world in terms of existing concepts, schema, and modes of thought by putting new information into existing mental frameworks is called: (8)

a.   accommodation
b.   assimilation
c.   conservation
d.   metacognition

8.   In Piaget's theory, knowledge that certain physical attributes of an object remain unchanged even though the outward appearance of the object is altered is called: (9)

a.   egocentrism
b.   object permanence
c.   assimilation
d.   conservation

9.   In research dealing with imaginary moral dilemmas, which involve completing courses of action, Kohlberg assessed level of moral development on the basis of: (12)

a.   subjects' selected course of action only
b.   subjects' selected course of action and explanations for their selected course of action
c.   subjects' explanation for their selected course of action only
d.   neither subjects' course of action nor explanation for their selected course of action

10.   In classifying temperament, children that are relatively inactive and apathetic and show mild negative reactions to many new situations or experiences are referred to as: (16)

a.   difficult children
b.   aggressive children
c.   slow-to-warm-up children
d.   unclassifiable children

CHAPTER 9

HUMAN DEVELOPMENT II:
ADOLESCENCE, ADULTHOOD, AND AGING

ADOLESCENCE: BETWEEN CHILD AND ADULT

1.   Define puberty. (336)

      Describe when adolescence has been traditionally viewed as beginning and ending. (336-337)

      a.   beginning

      b.   ending

2.   The beginning of adolescence is signaled by a sudden increase in the rate of physical growth. This growth spurt is just one aspect of the process of puberty. Another aspect of the process of puberty is achieving sexual maturity and becoming capable of reproduction. Describe the changes found in the development of sexual maturity for both males and females. Include information about hormonal changes and other changes which occur during this period. (337)

      a.   males

      b.   females

      Some individuals reach sexual maturity earlier than others. Describe the effects of early sexual maturation on both males and females. (338)

      a.   males

      b.   females

3.   Piaget believed that, in many ways, adolescents think and reason like adults. Describe three tasks that the adolescent can perform during the stage of formal operations. (338)

1.

2.

3.

The idea that adolescents' thinking is different from that of adults is supported by many theorists. Describe how the concepts of imaginary audience and personal fable are used by Elkind to explain the thought patterns of the adolescent. (338)

a.   imaginary audience

b.   personal fable

Define adolescent invulnerability (339)

List two factors that may contribute to adolescents engaging in high risk behavior. (339)

a.

b.

4.   There is evidence which shows that adolescents experience more frequent and more intense mood swings than do adults. Describe what has been discovered about adolescents with respect to the following areas of emotional development. (340)

a.   happiness and self-confidence

b.   relationships with parents

5.   Friendships become increasingly important during the period of adolescence. While friendships confer many important benefits (including a wide array of social skills and the capacity for intimacy), the potential negative effects of friendships can not be ignored. Describe the findings of two studies that have demonstrated that friendships can have a negative effect on the adolescent. (340-341)

    a.   Shantz and Hartup (1993)

    b.   Berndt (1992)

6.   Erik Erikson proposed a stage theory of human development that examines the entire lifespan. Briefly describe Erikson's theory. (341-343)

    List Erikson's eight stages of psychosocial development that coincide with the following developmental periods. (341-342; also see Key Concept 343)

    Infancy
            a.

    Childhood
            a.
            b.
            c.

    Adolescence
            a.

    . Adulthood
            a.
            b.
            c.

According to Erikson, adolescents enter the psychosocial stage of identity vs. role confusion. Describe the crisis that the adolescent has to resolve during this life stage. (341-342; also see Key Concept 343)

Describe three strategies that the adolescent adopts to help him/her resolve personal identity crises. (342)

a.

b.

c.

7.   It is commonly agreed that the adolescent of today faces a new and uniquely disturbing set of problems. Describe the effect that divorce, parent-absent, and blended families may have on the adolescent of today. (344-346)

a.   divorce

b.   parent-absent

c.   blended families

Define dysfunctional families. (345)

Describe how dysfunctional families can affect the adolescent of today. (345-346)

8.   Adolescents and their parents have generally displayed different attitudes toward sexuality. However, this "generation gap" appears to have narrowed. Describe what has been discovered in recent surveys about the attitudes of parents and adolescents regarding adolescent sexuality. (346)

    a.   adolescents' attitudes

    b.   parents' attitudes

9.   Large numbers of adolescents are at risk for psychological and physical harm. Yet despite the adverse conditions under which they grow up, many adolescents avoid potential harm and go on to lead productive lives. According to systematic research, what do parents do to help adolescents avoid potential harm? (347; also see the Point of It All)

ADULTHOOD AND AGING

10.   Psychologists who study adulthood tend to view the changes of this life stage from one of two perspectives. Describe the "crisis" (or "stage") approach of Erik Erikson and others. (348)

Erikson believes that there are three important stages of adult development. Name and briefly describe these three stages. (348-349)

a.

b.

c.

Describe a sharply different perspective on adult development, the "life event" (or "timing-of-life-event") model. (349)

11.   Physical change occurs gradually throughout the human life cycle. However, by mid-life physical changes are more abrupt. One of the most dramatic changes experienced by both women and men at mid-life is the climacteric. Describe the effects of the climacteric on women and men. (351)

   a.   women

   b.   men

   Describe the findings of research on the relationship between the experience of menopause and the role of cultural factors. (see Perspectives on Diversity 351-352)

   Some physical decline is inevitable during mid-life. However, growing evidence suggests that <u>other</u> factors may be better predictors of physical vigor and health, than biological age. List four factors. (352)

   a.

   b.

   c.

   d.

Describe the findings of systematic research on physical changes in later life among people who are in their sixties, seventies, and eighties. (353)

Not all physical change is due solely to growing older or primary aging. Some decline is due to secondary aging. Define secondary aging. (353)

List and describe four decrements in sensory abilities that can influence the driving ability of older adults. (353-354)

a.

b.

c.

d.

12.   Describe the conclusions of research regarding the following kinds of memory abilities of older and younger adults. (355)

a.   short-term memory

b.   long-term memory

c.   memory for meaningful information

d.   prospective memory

Describe the findings of Sinnott's (1986) research on memory for meaningful information among younger and older adults. (355)

Does prospective memory decline among older adults? (355)

Describe recent research on memory and age-related stereotypes. (356)

What do the findings of the May, Hasler, and Stoltzfus (1993) study indicate regarding the relationship among memory, aging, and circadian rhythms? (356; also see Figure 9.2)

Describe what is known about problem solving abilities and aging. (356)

Describe the findings of research on intelligence, wisdom, and creativity across the life span. (see the Research Process 357-359)

a.   intelligence

b.   wisdom

c.   creativity

13.   Levinson proposed a theory that attempts to explain adult social development. He believes that all adults pass through several transition periods as they move between distinct stages of their adult life. Describe the early adult transition period, in which we move from adolescence into adulthood. (359-361)

Describe the two key components of the life structure during early adulthood. (360)

a.   the dream

b.   the mentor

Describe the mid-life transition period, which for most people occurs between the ages of forty to forty-five. (360-361)

Describe the late-adult transition period, which occurs for most persons between the ages of sixty and sixty-five. (361)

14.   Contrast the findings of studies of couples who remain happily married versus couples who divorce. (362-363)

    a.   happily married couples

        1)
        2)
        3)
        4)
        5)
        6)
        7)

    b.   couples who are unhappy and/or divorce

        1)
        2)
        3)
        4)
        5)
        6)
        7)
        8)
        9)
      10)

15.   List and describe four findings of a longitudinal research study on the negative effects of unemployment. (364)

    a.

    b.

    c.

    d.

16.   Describe how women differ from men in the following areas of adult development. (364-365)

     a.   possessing a dream

     b.   forming a relationship with a mentor

     c.   mastery

     d.   pleasure

     e.   midlife crisis

AGING AND DEATH: THE END OF LIFE

17.   While many theories of aging have been proposed, most fall under one of two major headings: wear-and-tear theories and genetic theories. Describe the two wear-and-tear theories of aging. (365-366)

     a.

     b.

     Describe genetic-programming theories of aging. (366)

18.   Kubler-Ross has proposed that people who are faced with their impending death pass through a series of five stages. List the stages and describe the reactions of people in each of these five stages. (367)

     a.

     b.

     c.

     d.

e.

Describe the conclusion your textbook author reached after reviewing research on Kubler- Ross's theory of death and dying.

19.   List and describe the four stages of bereavement outlined in the textbook. (367-368)

a.

b.

c.

d.

MAKING PSYCHOLOGY A PART OF YOUR LIFE

20.   List four steps that can increase your chances of being successful in today's job market. (368-369)

a.

b.

c.

d.

CHAPTER NINE QUIZ

1. Adolescence is traditionally viewed as beginning with the: (1)

   a. onset of puberty
   b. ending of puberty
   c. entrance into high school
   d. establishment of gender identity

2. Research findings suggest that early sexual maturation is a(n) _____ for boys and a(n) _____ for girls: (2)

   a. disadvantage; disadvantage
   b. disadvantage; advantage
   c. advantage; advantage
   d. advantage; disadvantage

3. According to Elkind, adolescents' belief that their feelings and thoughts are totally unique is called: (3)

   a. the personal fable
   b. egocentrism
   c. animism
   d. secondary aging

4. Research results best support which of the following statements: (4)

   a. Teenagers experience wider and faster mood swings than adults.
   b. The majority of teenagers report feeling unhappy or distressed.
   c. Most teenagers disagree with parents on issues related to basic values.
   d. All of the other alternative statements are supported by research results.

5. According to Erikson, an understanding of an individual's unique traits and what is really of central importance to them is called: (6)

   a. crystallized intelligence
   b. fluid intelligence
   c. life structure
   d. self-identity

6. The two major approaches to adult development include: (10)

   a. crisis or stage approach and life event approach
   b. fluid approach and crystallized approach
   c. dysfunctional approach and autonomy approach
   d. transition approach and maturation approach

7.   Erikson's second crisis of adult life centers around an individual's ability to overcome selfish, self-centered concerns and to take an active interest in helping and guiding the next generation. The stage where this crisis occurs is referred to as: (10)

a.   intimacy versus isolation
b.   autonomy versus shame and doubt
c.   integrity versus despair
d.   generativity versus self-absorption

8.   In the terminology of life events models of adults development, graduation from school would be an example of: (10)

a.   an internal crisis
b.   a normative event
c.   a non-normative event
d.   a social clock

9.   With respect to short-term memory, older persons in comparison to young adults have a: (12)

a.   slightly greater capacity
b.   slightly smaller capacity
c.   similar capacity
d.   extremely smaller capacity

10. According to Levinson, two key components influencing an individual's views about the nature of his or her life are: (13)

a.   trust and mistrust
b.   autonomy and intimacy
c.   wish fulfillment and transference
d.   dream and mentor

CHAPTER 10

MOTIVATION AND EMOTION

MOTIVATION: THE ACTIVATION AND PERSISTENCE OF BEHAVIOR

1.   Motivation is an internal process that activates and guides overt behavior. Psychologists are interested in what makes people act or perform in a given manner. Several theories of motivation have been offered by psychologists. Discuss the basic assumptions (beliefs) underlying each of the theories of motivation presented in the textbook. (375-379)

    a.   instinct theory

    b.   drive theory

    c.   arousal theory

    d.   expectancy theory

    e.   Maslow's Hierarchy of Needs

    Describe how expectancy theory can be used to explain work motivation. (378)

2.   Hunger is a powerful motive. How much we eat is determined by both internal and external factors. Describe the internal and external factors that are involved in regulating eating. (380-381)

    a.   internal (e.g., special detectors)

    b.   external (e.g., smell, taste, sight, and culture)

3.   Why do some people have difficulty in maintaining their body weight? Identify and describe four factors. (381-382)

    a.

    b.

    c.

    d.

4.   Contrast the eating disorders of Anorexia Nervosa and Bulimia. (382-383)

List three points derived from research regarding anorexia and bulimia. (383-384; also see Figure 10.5)

a.

b.

c.

SEXUAL MOTIVATION: THE MOST INTIMATE MOTIVE

5.   Describe the relationship between sex hormones and human sexual behavior. (385)

Describe the role of other chemical substances in the body and human sexuality. (385-386)

6.   Describe the four phases of the human sexual response according to Masters and Johnson. (386-387)

a.   excitement phase

b.   plateau phase

c.   orgasmic phase

     d.   resolution phase

Are these phases universal? (387)

7.   List the four (4) factors that appear to arouse the human sexual response. (387-388)

     a.

     b.

     c.

     d.

8.   Define sexual jealousy. (388)

Buss and his colleagues (1992) found that there were gender differences in sexual jealousy. Describe these gender differences. (388-389; also see Figure 10.6)

     a.   female sexual jealousy

     b.   male sexual jealousy

9.   Recent evidence suggests that genetic factors may play a role in homosexuality. Describe the findings of a study, conducted by the National Cancer Institute's Laboratory of Biochemistry. (390-391)

Can we conclude that homosexuality is genetically determined or stems from genetic factors only? Explain your answer. (391)

AGGRESSIVE MOTIVATION: THE MOST DANGEROUS MOTIVE

10.   Freud and Lorenz believed that aggression was an inherited human tendency. What do present day psychologists believe? (391)

A wide range of social, environmental, and personal factors can influence aggression. One variable that has often been suggested as an important cause of aggressive motivation is frustration. Describe how frustration can influence aggression. (392)

Define frustration (392)

Define the frustration-aggression hypothesis. (392)

Does frustration always lead to aggression? (392)

List four other possible causes for aggression.

a.

b.

c.

d.

11.   Describe the role culture plays in expressions of aggression. (393-394; also see Figure 10.7)

ACHIEVEMENT AND POWER: TWO COMPLEX HUMAN MOTIVES

12.   Define achievement motivation. (394)

Define power motivation. (394)

Describe how achievement and power motivation are measured. (395)

Describe the life experiences of persons who are high and low in achievement motivation and power motivation. (395)

Describe Horner's research on gender differences in achievement motivation, and describe conclusions drawn from recent research. (395-396)

Do gender differences in achievement motivation really exist?

13.   Define intrinsic motivation. (396)

External rewards can sometimes reduce intrinsic motivation. However, this is not always true. Describe the conditions under which external rewards can enhance intrinsic motivation. (396-397; also see The Point of It All)

EMOTIONS: THEIR NATURE, EXPRESSION, AND IMPACT

14.   Contrast the Cannon-Bard and James-Lange theories of emotions. (399; also see Key Concept 401)

   a.   Cannon-Bard

   b.   James-Lange

15.   Describe Schachter and Singer's Two-Factor theory of human emotions. (400; also see Key Concept 401)

16.   Describe the two central assumptions of the opponent-process theory of emotion. (400-402)

   a.

   b.

17.   Research findings suggest that the cerebral hemispheres show a degree of specialization with respect to emotions. Describe the relationship between emotional expression and the two hemispheres of the cerebral cortex. (402-403)

   a.   left hemisphere

   b.   right hemisphere

18.   List three reasons why there are grounds for doubt about whether lie detectors can detect lies.

   a.

   b.

   c.

   What do lie detectors really measure? (403)

   Where is the use of lie detectors permissible, and where is it banned? (403-404)

   a.

   b.

THE EXTERNAL EXPRESSION OF EMOTION:
OUTWARD SIGNS OF INNER FEELINGS

19.   Define nonverbal cues. (404)

List the four ways others' emotions are revealed by nonverbal cues. (404-407)

a.

b.

c.

d.

20.   Describe four ways in which our affect (mood) influences cognition (how we process information about ourselves or the external world). (407-408)

a.

b.

c.

d.

21.   Are people in a good mood easier to influence? Describe the findings of Mackie and Worth's (1989) research on this topic. (See the Research Process and Figure 10.8)

22.   Describe the four (4) ways in which cognition influence affect. (410)

a.

b.

c.

d.

Making Psychology a Part of Your Life

23.   List the six (6) guidelines for setting and achieving goals. (411)

      a.

      b.

      c.

      d.

      e.

      f.

CHAPTER TEN QUIZ

1.   Which of the following theories suggests that motivation is basically a process in which various biological needs push or drive us to actions designed to satisfy these biological needs?: (1)

    a.   drive theory
    b.   instinct theory
    c.   expectancy theory
    d.   intrinsic motivation theory

2.   Which of the following best represents expectancy theory?: (1)

    a.   Learning how to dance in order to improve your social life.
    b.   Reading novels in order to improve your exam scores for entrance exams into graduate school.
    c.   Working overtime without pay in the hope that it will lead to a promotion.
    d.   All of the other alternatives are equally likely to be explained on the basis of expectancy theory.

3.   Obese individuals differ from non-obese in that obese individuals are: (3)

    a.   likely to decrease their intake of food during stress
    b.   likely to feel hungrier when exposed to food-related cues, for example, smells of food
    c.   not influenced by external cues relating to food
    d.   characterized by none of the other alternatives

4.   According to Masters and Johnson, the greatest differences between males and females in the four phases of sexual behavior is in the: (6)

    a.   orgasmic phases
    b.   plateau phase
    c.   resolution phase
    d.   refractory phase

5.   Frustration is most likely to lead to aggression when it is viewed: (10)

    a.   only as unfair
    b.   only as unexpected
    c.   as neither unfair nor unexpected
    d.   as either unfair or unexpected

6.   The desire to meet standards of excellence--to outperform others and accomplish difficult tasks--is called: (12)

    a.   achievement motivation
    b.   power motivation
    c.   excellence motivation
    d.   thematic motivation

7. Intrinsically motivated behaviors are most likely to be reinforced by such things as: (13)

    a. expectations of later monetary rewards
    b. fear of punishment
    c. avoidance of an unpleasant event
    d. a feeling of accomplishment

8. The theory of emotion that asserts that different patterns of emotional activity are associated with different emotions is the: (14)

    a. Cannon-Bard theory
    b. James-Lange theory
    c. Schachter-Singer theory
    d. facial feedback theory

9. Opponent process theory assumes that repeated exposure to a stimulus causes the initial reaction to _____ and the opponent process to _____. (16)

    a. strengthen; weaken
    b. weaken; strengthen
    c. weaken; weaken
    d. strengthen; strengthen

10. Outward signs of others' emotional states, for example, facial expressions, are called: (19)

    a. unconditioned responses
    b. nonverbal cues
    c. conditioned responses
    d. display rules

CHAPTER 11

INDIVIDUAL DIFFERENCES I:
INTELLIGENCE, GENDER

ITS NATURE AND MEASUREMENT

1.   Define intelligence. (416)

2.   Historically, psychologists have offered different perspectives on the nature of intelligence. Some have perceived intelligence as a single characteristic while others have perceived intelligence as multifaceted. Still others have proposed a more integrated view of intelligence. Describe these three views of intelligence by summarizing what each of the following psychologists proposed: (417)

      a.   Spearman

      b.   Thurstone

      c.   Cattell

What do most psychologists believe about the nature of intelligence today? (418)

3.   Robert Sternberg's theory of intelligence is representative of the information processing approach to examining intelligence. Describe Sternberg's triarchic theory of intelligence and give an example of each of the three types of intelligence. (418; and see Figure 11.1)

    a.   componential intelligence

        example:

    b.   experiential intelligence

        example:

    c.   contextual intelligence

        example:

4.   Describe the neuroscience approach to examining intelligence. (418-419)

Describe the findings/results of studies that support the neuroscience approach to examining intelligence. (419-420)

    a.   Reed and Jensen (1993)

    b.   Haier et al. (in press)

    c.   Andreasen et al. (1993)

5.   Alfred Binet and Theodore Simon developed the first psychological test of intelligence.
      Describe the underlying assumption (belief) that guided the development of the Binet-
      Simon test. (421)

      Describe why this was an important assumption. (421)

6.   What did the letters I Q stand for originally? (421)

      In arriving at an IQ score, how is a "mental" age computed?

      How did psychologists compute an IQ score initially? (421)

      Discuss at least one obvious flaw in computing IQ scores. (421)

      What does IQ mean today? (421-422)

7.   The Wechsler Scales are tests for both children and adults that are among the most
      frequently used individual intelligence tests today. Describe how the Wechsler Scales
      differ from the earlier versions of the Stanford-Binet test. (422-423; and see Figure 11.4
      and Table 11.1)

Describe how it is used diagnostically. (422-423)

a.

b.

How accurate is it as a diagnostic test? (423)

a.   for the WAIS

b.   for the WISC

8.   Why were group tests of intelligence developed? (424)

Describe the Army Alpha and the Army Beta group tests of intelligence. (424)

9.   According to Baron (1995), there are at least two basic requirements of a psychological test: a psychological test must have reliability and validity. A psychological test has reliability if it yields the same score or value every time it is given. Describe the procedures used to determine split-half and test-retest reliability. (424-425; also see Figure 11.5)

a.   split-half reliability

b.   test-retest reliability

10.　A psychological test has validity if it measures what it claims it measures. There are at least three types of validity that psychologists feel are important: content, criterion-related, and construct. What do these three types of validity tell us about a psychological test? Give an example of each. (425-426; also see Key Concept 428)

　　a.　content validity

　　　　example:

　　b.　criterion-related

　　　　example:

　　c.　construct

　　　　example:

11.　Why might ethnic and racial minorities score lower on group tests of intelligence than whites of European ancestry?

Helms (1992) notes that widely used intelligence tests also suffer from other forms of cultural bias that are not as apparent but just as damaging for minority children. Describe this more subtle form of cultural bias in intelligence testing that exists in mainstream American culture. (427-429)

What is the rationale or purpose of a culture-fair test of intelligence? (429; and see Figure 11.6)

What does Baron (1995) suggest as a possible solution to designing a culture-fair test of intelligence? (430)

12.   Individual tests of intelligence may be used to determine mental retardation and intellectual giftedness. Describe two (2) factors that determine degrees of retardation. (The Point of It All - 430-431; and see Figure 11.7)

a.

b.

Describe two (2) possible causes of mental retardation. (The Point of It All - 430-431)

a.

b.

What have individual tests of intelligence taught us about the lives of the intellectually gifted? (The Point of It All - 431)

Why does Resnick (1993) feel that intellectual gifted children in America and elsewhere are being ignored? (The Point of It All - 431-432)

HUMAN INTELLIGENCE: THE ROLE OF HEREDITY AND THE ROLE OF ENVIRONMENT

13.   Research supports the view that heredity plays a role in human intelligence. For example, the more closely two persons are related, the more similar their IQs will be. How similar are the IQ scores of identical twins reared together? (432; and see Figure 11.8)

What have studies of adopted children taught us about the nature of intelligence? (433)

What have the results of the Minnesota Study of Twins Raised Apart taught us? (433)

Can we conclude that genes play a more important role in determining intellectual capability than the environment? (434)

14.   Describe what environmental deprivation and environmental enrichment studies reveal about the nature of intelligence. (435-436)

What has research on birth order and intelligence taught us? (436; and see Figure 11.9)

List other environmental factors that have been found to be related to IQ scores. (436-437)

a.

b.

c.

15.   What role has the field of behavioral genetics played in shaping our understanding of the nature of intelligence? (437)

GENDER: HOW MALES AND FEMALES DIFFER

16.   Define gender. (438)

17.   Describe how males and females differ with respect to sending and receiving nonverbal cues. (439)

a.   males

b.   females

How do gender stereotypes influence emotional expression in males and females? (439)

a.   females

b.   males

18.   Describe three factors that might account for why females appear to be influenced to a greater extent by evaluative feedback than do males. (440; and see Figure 11.10)

        a.

        b.

        c.

19.   Research suggests that male and female leaders appear to differ in a few respects, but these differences are small in magnitude. However, research does support the view that males and females are evaluated differently. Summarize the findings of Eagly and her colleagues (1992) concerning this issue. (441-442)

20.   Gender role stereotypes support the notion that males are more aggressive than females. However, current research suggest that males are not more aggressive than females if you consider the form of aggression and the context of aggression. Summarize the findings of studies that suggest males and females differ with respect to the use of indirect and direct aggression. (442-443; and see Figure 11.11)

21.   Elkins and Peterson (1993) asked male and female students to describe their relationships with their actual best friends and with what would be their ideal best friend. Describe the findings of their study. (443-444)

22.   Describe how the parental investment model explains mate selection decisions of men and women. (444-445)

   a.   men

   b.   women

23.   Describe the matching hypothesis as it relates to mate selection. (445-446; and see the Research Process)

Do males and females show equal degrees of matching for long-term relationships, but different degrees of matching for one-night stands? Explain. (446; and see Figure 11.12)

Describe how males and females rate physical attractiveness. (447; and see Figure 11.13)

24.   Describe the findings of research that suggests that males and females differ with respect to their sexual attitudes and beliefs. (447-449)

males

females

25.   Research indicates that there are gender differences with respect to psychological adjustment. Describe what is known about gender differences and psychological adjustment in the following three areas: (449-450)

a.   depression

b.   mathematics anxiety

c.   sex-typed vs. androgynous

26.   Describe what is known about the relationship between gender differences and cognitive abilities. (450-451; and see Table 11.2)

27.   Describe how the socialization process influences gender differences in male and female children. (451; and see Figure 11.14)

28.   Describe the potential role of biological factors in gender difference between males and females. (452-453; and see Figure 11.15

CHAPTER ELEVEN QUIZ

1. According to Spearman, our ability to perform any and all cognitive tasks is most dependent on: (2)

    a. crystallized intelligence
    b. fluid intelligence
    c. s factor
    d. g factor

2. In Sternberg's triarchic theory, the type of intelligence that involves the ability to quickly recognize what factors influence success on various tasks and is adept at both adapting to and shaping the environment is called: (3)

    a. componential intelligence
    b. contextual intelligence
    c. fluid intelligence
    d. experiential intelligence

3. For what purpose was the original device for measuring human intelligence developed by Binet and Simon?: (5)

    a. to develop a unified measure of intelligence
    b. to identify children who should acquire a post-secondary education
    c. to identify children who were mentally retarded and would not benefit from regular education
    d. it was developed for all the reasons listed in the other alternatives

4. Originally, IQ scores were obtained by dividing _____ age by _____ and multiplying by 100. (6)

    a. mental, chronological
    b. chronological, mental
    c. general, specific
    d. specific, general

5. Dividing a test into two halves in order to determine whether individuals attained equivalent scores on the two halves is called: (9)

    a. test-retest validity
    b. concurrent validity
    c. predictive reliability
    d. split-half reliability

6.   Tests determining whether a person should become a licensed psychologist need to contain questions related to skills used by competent psychologists. Tests that accomplish this are said to have good: (10)

      a.   test-retest reliability
      b.   concurrent validity
      c.   content validity
      d.   split-half reliability

7.   The more closely two people are related, the _____ their IQ's: (13)

      a.   lower
      b.   higher
      c.   more similar
      d.   more different

8.   With respect to emotional expression and gender differences, females are expected to express more positive emotions about: (17)

      a.   themselves
      b.   accomplishments
      c.   others
      d.   as equally as males for all of the other alternatives

9.   Which of the following is most supported by research findings? (20)

      a.   males show fewer forms of direct aggression than females
      b.   males show more forms of direct aggression than females
      c.   males and females express direct aggression equally often
      d.   males and females express indirect aggression equally often

10.   The view that people seek to attain romantic partners that are at least as desirable as themselves is called: (23)

      a.   prenatal investment mode
      b.   equity theory
      c.   matching hypothesis
      d.   competition hypothesis

CHAPTER 12

INDIVIDUAL DIFFERENCES II:
PERSONALITY — CONSISTENCY IN THE BEHAVIOR OF INDIVIDUALS

1.　　Define personality. (460)

Some psychologists argue that people demonstrate consistency in their behavior across different situations and over long periods of time. Others argue that behavior is largely determined by external factors rather than by stable traits or dispositions. Describe what most psychologists now agree on regarding these two arguments. (460-461)

THE PSYCHOANALYTIC APPROACH:
MESSAGES FROM THE UNCONSCIOUS

2.　　There are four topics that are central to Freud's theory of personality: levels of consciousness, the structure of personality, anxiety and defense mechanisms, and the psychosexual stages of development.

　　　List and describe the three levels of consciousness. (462-463, and see Fig. 12.1)

　　　a.

　　　b.

　　　c.

3. Describe the three structures of the personality, including the principles under which they operate. For each, indicate the level(s) of consciousness at which it functions. (463-464; and see Fig. 12.1)

    a.   id

    b.   ego

    c.   superego

4. Describe the function of the defense mechanisms. (465)

    List the defense mechanisms and describe them. (488-489; and see Table 12.1)

    a.

    b.

    c.

    d.

    e.

    f.

g.

5.   Define libido and fixation. (466)

a.   libido

b.   fixation

Explain Freud's view of Psychosexual Stages of Development, considered to be one of the most controversial aspects of his theory. (466; and see Fig. 12.2)

List and describe the psychosexual stages of development that occur at approximately the following ages. Include the results of fixation in the oral and anal stages. (466-467; and see Fig. 12.2)

a.   0-2 years old

b.   2-3 years old

c.   3-7 years old

d.   7-11 years old

e.   11 years - adult

Define the terms Oedipus Complex, penis envy, and Freudian slips. (466-448)

a.   Oedipus Complex

b.   penis envy

c.   Freudian slips

6.   State four criticisms of Freud's theory. (468-469)

a.

b.

c.

d.

Even though many psychologists accept only some aspects of Freud's theory, what does your author feel was Freud's contribution to psychology? (469)

How do cultural differences concerning the nature and expression of love and intimacy relate to Freud's theory? (469-470)

OTHER PSYCHOANALYTIC VIEWS:
FREUD'S DISCIPLES . . . AND DISSENTERS

7.   Explain the term neo-Freudian.

       Summarize the neo-Freudian positions of Jung, Horney, and Adler. (471-474; see Key
       People)

       a.   Jung's position

       b.   Horney's position

       c.   Alder's position

HUMANISTIC THEORIES: EMPHASIS ON GROWTH

8.   Contrast the Freudian and Humanistic views about what is necessary to function as
       healthy rational adults. List the three characteristics shared by the humanistic theories.
       (475)

       a.   Freudian view

       b.   Humanistic view

       c.   three characteristics

              1)

              2)

              3)

9.   Compare Rogers's "full-functioning person" with Maslow's concept of "self-actualizing people". What explanation did Rogers offer for our failure to succeed as full-functioning people, and what can be done about it? (476-477)

   a.   full-functioning person

   b.   self-actualizing people

   c.   Rogers's explanation

   d.   what can be done about it (include in your answer the term "unconditional positive regard.")

10.   State three criticisms of Humanistic Theory. (478)

   a.

   b.

   c.

11.   Define self-disclosure. (478; and see The Research Process)

   Describe the stranger-on-the-bus effect. (479)

   Describe the relationship between self-disclosure and psychological health. (479-480)

TRAIT THEORIES: SEEKING THE KEY DIMENSIONS OF PERSONALITY

12.   Describe the basic idea behind the trait theory approach to personality development. After reading the sections on Allport's and Cattell's theories, list the five key or central dimensions of personality. (480-485)

   a.   trait theory

   b.   central dimensions

      1)
      2)
      3)
      4)
      5)

   List two criticisms of trait theory

   a.

   b.

LEARNING APPROACHES TO PERSONALITY

13.   Contrast the way Freud and the behavioral and social learning approach explained the consistency and uniqueness found in personality. (484)

   a.   Freud

   b.   behavioral and social learning approach

14.   Note that radical behaviorism (Skinner) denied the importance of internal causes of
       behavior, such as motives, traits, intentions, desires, etc. Bandura's Social Cognitive
       Theory did not agree with Skinner. Define social cognitive theory and two of Bandura's
       concepts: **self-reinforcement** and **self-efficacy**. (485)

       a.   social cognitive theory

       b.   self-reinforcement

       c.   self-efficacy

15.   Rotter has proposed a theory on locus of control, i.e. a person's perceived location of
       control of their destiny. Describe internals and externals. (486)

       a.   internals

       b.   externals

KEY ASPECTS OF PERSONALITY: A SAMPLE OF RECENT RESEARCH

16.   List seven behaviors that are more likely to be displayed by people with high self
       esteem. (488-490)

       a.

       b.

       c.

       d.

e.

f.

Describe a negative effect caused by high self-esteem.

Describe the differences between high and low self-monitoring. Where do you fit? (490-491, see Key Principle)

a.   high self-monitoring

b.   low self-monitoring

c.   where you fit

18.   Describe the sensation seeking personality. (492)

Describe a possible biological basis for the sensation seeking personality (492).

List four characteristics of sensation seekers. (492-493)

CHAPTER 12 QUIZ

1.   According to Freud, the part of the mind that contains the impulses of which we are not aware is the: (2)

    a.   conscious
    b.   preconscious
    c.   unconscious
    d.   subconscious

2.   According to Freud, the part of our personality that functions on the basis on the reality principle is: (3)

    a.   the id
    b.   the ego
    c.   the superego
    d.   the conscious

3.   A defense mechanism that channels unacceptable impulses into socially acceptable action is called: (4)

    a.   reaction formation
    b.   repression
    c.   regression
    d.   sublimation

4.   Which of the following is the correct order of Freud's stages of psychosexual development? (5)

    a.   oral, anal, phallic, latency, genital
    b.   oral, phallic, anal, sexual, genital
    c.   oral, anal, genital, sexual, phallic
    d.   oral, sexual, phallic, latency, genital

5.   The neo-Freudian who proposed the existence of the collective unconscious was: (7)

    a.   Adler
    b.   Jung
    c.   Horney
    d.   Fromm

6.   The humanistic theorists emphasize: (8)

    a.   early development
    b.   personal responsibility
    c.   the unconscious
    d.   learning

7.   According to Rogers, to become a full-functioning person requires: (9)

      a.   conditional regard
      b.   environmental blocking
      c.   control of emotions
      d.   unconditional positive regard

8.   Which of the following is one of the three criticisms of Humanistic Theory? (10)

      a.   too much emphasis on observable behavior
      b.   too much emphasis on the unconscious
      c.   their assumptions about human nature are overly optimistic
      d.   too much emphasis on determinism

9.   Which of the following is not one of the five key dimensions of personality identified by recent research? (12)

      a.   extroversion
      b.   agreeableness
      c.   intelligence
      d.   conscientiousness

10.   When compared to low sensation-seekers, high-sensation seekers (18)

      a.   have less ability to ignore irrelevant information
      b.   show weaker orienting responses to the initial presentation of an unfamiliar auditory stimulus
      c.   have lower levels of endorphins
      d.   are characterized by all the above

CHAPTER 13

HEALTH, STRESS, AND COPING

HEALTH PSYCHOLOGY: AN OVERVIEW

1.   Define health psychology. Health psychology reflects the view that what two factors combine to be important determinants of health and illness? (501)

      a.   health psychology

      b.   two factors:

            1)   2)

2.   A majority of the conditions that now constitute the leading causes of death in our country could be prevented if people would do five things. List these five things below. (501)

      a.

      b.

      c.

      d.

      e.

STRESS: ITS CAUSES, EFFECTS, AND CONTROL

3.   Define stress. (503) (use glossary)

4.   Many events have the potential to cause stress in our lives, but those with the greatest potential to cause stress share three characteristics. List these three characteristics: (503)

     a.

     b.

     c.

5.   Hans Selye has developed a model of the physiological reactions experienced by a person exposed to prolonged and severe stress. This sequence of bodily reactions is called the <u>general adaptation syndrome</u> (GAS). List and describe the three stages of the GAS. (503-504, 507)

     a.

     b.

     c.

     Describe our body's resistance to stressful events during each of these stages (503-504; and see Figure 13.2)

     a.   alarm stage

     b.   resistance stage

     c.   exhaustion stage

6.   Selye's model fails to take into account our cognitive appraisal of potentially stressful events. Describe two important cognitive appraisals that determine whether a particular situation will be experienced as stressful. (504-505, and 507)

     a.

     b.

7.   One potential source of stress is exposure to a number of <u>stressful life events</u> over a 12 - 18 month period. Describe the general conclusions regarding the relationship between stressful events and health. (506-509)

8.   Another potential source of stress is repeated exposure to <u>daily hassles</u> - events which are not extreme but which, nevertheless, have the potential to frustrate us. Describe what a 1992 study discovered about the number of daily hassles experienced by a native-American population as a predictor of later health. (509)

Explain why your author concludes that, for some people, the minor hassles of everyday life are even more detrimental to health than are major life events. (509)

9.   Environmental disasters can also serve as a source of stress. In extreme cases, these disasters can cause victims to experience a post-traumatic stress disorder. This disorder is a reaction that can occur as long as years after a traumatic event. Victims of incest or violent crime and veterans of the Viet Nam war often experience this disorder. Describe the characteristics of the post-traumatic stress disorder. (510)

10.   A fourth potential source of stress is work-related stress. Figure 13.4 in your textbook shows some of the major sources of work-related stress. Describe each of the following factors, which have been shown to be related to work-related stress. (511)

a.   work-overload

b.   work-underload

c.   role-conflict

d.   performance appraisals

11.   Your author describes several methods by which employers can help to reduce
        work-related stress. One method is to be aware of the fit between a worker's personal
        traits and the environmental demands of a job - the P(erson)-E(nvironmental) Fit.
        Describe two other ways employers can help to reduce work-related stress. (512-513)

        a.

        b.

12.   Stress has been implicated in the occurrence of a number of diseases. Describe
        possible means by which stress is related to these disorders. (514)

13.   It has been discovered that even low or moderate levels of stress may interfere with
        our ability to perform various tasks. Describe two reasons why this is true. (515)

        a.

        b.

14.   Some persons suffer from such a high level of work-related stress that they experience
        burnout. List and describe four characteristics of burnout. (515; and see Figure 13.6)

        a.

        b.

        c.

        d.

        Describe two possible job-related outcomes when burnout occurs. (516)

        a.

        b.

15. Different people respond to stress in different ways. Describe how optimists and pessimists are affected differently by stress. (517)

Describe three strategies that optimists tend to adopt when dealing with stressful situations. (517, table 13.2)

a.

b.

c.

Describe hardiness. (518, use glossary) Underline the three C's in the definition which are characteristics of hardiness.

UNDERSTANDING AND COMMUNICATING OUR HEALTH NEEDS

16. The health-belief model describes two factors that often interact to determine whether or not we will seek medical advice or help for unusual physical symptoms. Describe these two factors. (519; and see Figure 13. 7)

a.

b.

BEHAVIORAL AND PSYCHOLOGICAL CORRELATES OF ILLNESS: THE EFFECTS OF THOUGHTS AND ACTIONS ON HEALTH

17. Smoking has been proven to be the leading cause of several types of cancer. Describe three reasons why people continue to smoke in spite of the risks associated with smoking. (523-524)

a.

b.

c.

Provide information about the effects of nicotine upon concentration, recall, alertness, etc. (523-524)

Worldwide, the greatest increase in smoking-related deaths is expected to occur among United States women. Describe two reasons why this is so. (525-526)

a.

b.

18.   Describe one dietary factor shown to increase the risk of breast cancer, and show how it is related to menopause. (526-527)

Describe one dietary factor which has been shown to reduce the risk of breast cancer. (527)

19.   Diet is also a factor in the development of cardiovascular disease. List and describe the three major cardiovascular diseases. (527)

a.

b.

c.

Describe the cause of arteriosclerosis. (527)

Show how serum cholesterol can be reduced, lowering the risk of arteriosclerosis. (527)

20.   In addition to smoking and diet, describe how alcohol consumption can be a significant factor in our health. Describe how even moderate levels of alcohol consumption have been shown to be directly related to our risk of developing certain kinds of cancer. (527-528)

21.   Even our emotions can play a role in the progression of both cancer and hypertension (high blood pressure). List below the two emotional responses which show the strongest relationship with high blood pressure. (528)

        a.

        b.

22.   Describe the "Type A" behavior pattern. (528)

        Describe the impact of this behavior pattern on the work situation. (528)

        Describe the three factors of the Type A behavior pattern recent research has shown to be the most likely to lead to the development of cardiovascular disease. (529)

        a.

        b.

        c.

23.   List the name of the virus that leads to AIDS.

        List the two primary ways by which AIDS can be spread. (530)

        a.

        b.

        Complete the following statement. (531)

        Worldwide, AIDS is being spread mainly through _____ _____ intercourse, rather than through unprotected homosexual intercourse.

Describe what is, at present, the only effective means of combatting AIDS. (531)

Describe psychology's role in AIDS prevention. (532)

Describe three beliefs held by adolescents that makes it more likely that they will engage in the consistent use of condoms during their sexual encounters. (531)

a.

b.

c.

PROMOTING WELLNESS: DEVELOPING A HEALTHIER LIFE STYLE

24. Studies of individuals who live to be more than one hundred years old show that some behaviors may actually increase life expectancy. List four of these behaviors. (533)

a.

b.

c.

d.

25. Prevention strategies are techniques designed to reduce the occurrence of illness and the accompanying physical and psychological problems. List and briefly describe two types of prevention strategies. (533)

a.

b.

26. Mass media attempts to persuade people to adopt healthier life styles have normally not been very successful. Describe one reason why this is true. (534)

The mass media, however, can be an effective tool for promoting healthy behavioral changes when combined with another factor. List that factor below.

27.   Regular exercise promotes both physical and mental health and reduces the risks
       from a number of illnesses. Describe three suggestions designed to increase the
       probability that we will maintain a regular exercise program. (535-536)

       a.

       b.

       c.

MAKING PSYCHOLOGY PART OF YOUR LIFE
MANAGING STRESS: SOME USEFUL TACTICS

28.   Describe the following techniques, which can be used to help us manage stress more
       effectively. (537-538)

       a.   progressive relaxation

       b.   time-management techniques

       c.   cognitive restructuring

       List the seven basic principles of effective time management. (538)

       a.

       b.

       c.

       d.

       e.

       f.

       g.

CHAPTER 13 QUIZ

1.   Those events that have the greatest potential to cause stress in our lives have all of
       the following in common <u>except</u>: (4)

       a.   uncontrollability
       b.   adaptability
       c.   overload
       d.   a tendency to evoke incompatible tendencies

2.   Susceptibility to illness increases most dramatically in the _____ stage of
       the general adaptation syndrome. (5)

       a.   alarm
       b.   terminal
       c.   resistance
       d.   exhaustion

3.   The term that refers to the frequently occurring, repetitive sources of stress that
       happen to us on an almost daily basis is: (8)

       a.   overload
       b.   burnout
       c.   hassles
       d.   stressors

4.   Survivors of devastating events often experience severe psychological problems
       called: (9)

       a.   schizophrenia
       b.   hassles
       c.   phobias
       d.   post-traumatic stress disorder

5.   Stress produces its damaging effects on our physical health by: (12)

       a.   interfering with the efficient operation of our immune system
       b.   disrupting a series of brain structures, especially the thalamus
       c.   elevating our blood pressure, which in turn causes other problems
       d.   disrupting our daily routines for such basic behaviors as sleeping and eating

6.   Which of the following describes a strategy for coping with stress preferred by
       optimists? (15)

       a.   refusing to believe that a problem exists
       b.   focusing on the expression of feelings, rather than working on the problem
              itself
       c.   giving up on reaching goals which involve some stress
       d.   making specific plans for dealing with the source of stress

7.   _____ is (are) the major cause of heart disease in the United States, and is (are) caused by the _____.(19)

    a.   deteriorating heart valves; lack of exercise
    b.   arteriosclerosis; lack of exercise
    c.   deteriorating heart valves; build up of cholesterol
    d.   arteriosclerosis; build up of cholesterol

8.   The characteristic of the Type A behavior pattern that has the strongest relationship with the risk of heart disease is: (22)

    a.   hurrying
    b.   impatience with the pace of other persons
    c.   cynical hostility
    d.   perfectionism

9.   Worldwide, AIDS is spread mainly through _____intercourse. (23)

    a.   male homosexual
    b.   female homosexual
    c.   heterosexual
    d.   both male and female homosexual

10.   Secondary prevention strategies involve: (25)

    a.   education about the relationship between health and behaviors
    b.   early detection
    c.   modifying poor health habits
    d.   promoting healthier life styles

CHAPTER 14

PSYCHOLOGICAL DISORDERS:
THEIR NATURE AND CAUSES

1. List four characteristics found, in varying degrees, among all of the psychological disorders. (544)

    a.

    b.

    c.

    d.

CHANGING CONCEPTIONS OF PSYCHOLOGICAL DISORDERS:
A BRIEF HISTORICAL PERSPECTIVE

2. Describe the way abnormal behavior was conceptualized in each of the following time periods: (545-546)

    a.   Earliest written history

    b.   Ancient Greek

    c.   Following the fall of the Roman empire

    d.   Following the renaissance, up to modern times

3. Define the medical perspective. (546)

Describe the relationship between the medical perspective and psychiatry. (546)

Contrast the psychiatric and psychological views regarding abnormal behavior. (546-547)

4. In the following chart, explain the psychodynamic perspective on mental disorders. In your explanation, include the following: unconscious urges, struggle, id, ego, and superego. Explain what Freud felt caused mental disorders to arise, and discuss how acceptable his views are today. (547)

Psychodynamic Perspective	
Cause	
Acceptance of this view	

5. List and give examples of the three factors most psychologists take into account when they attempt to understand the causes of abnormal behavior. (547-549, and see figure 14.1)

    a.

    b.

    c.

IDENTIFYING PSYCHOLOGICAL DISORDERS:
THE DSM-IV

6. Name the guide (manual) used by practitioners to identify specific disorders. (549)

    Describe the features of the DSM-IV. (549)

    a.

    b.

    c.

    d.

    e.

    Describe how the DSM-IV differs from earlier versions. (549-550)

    a.

    b.

    c.

Discuss the one thing the DSM does not attempt to do. (552)

Describe the two ways the DSM-IV attempts to take cultural factors into account. (552)

a.

b.

MOOD DISORDERS:
THE UPS AND DOWNS OF LIFE

7.   Define mood disorders. (554)

Describe the major symptoms of the two types of mood disorders listed below:

a.   depressive disorders

1)

2)

3)

4)

b.   bipolar disorders

8.   Describe how depressive disorders and bipolar disorders differ. (554)

Which type of mood disorder is more likely to be experienced by women?

9.   Depression has biological and psychological roots. Summarize research which points
      to the following causes of depression. (555-556)

      a.   genetics

      b.   abnormalities and brain biochemistry

      c.   learned helplessness

      d.   attribution

      e.   negative views

      f.   faulty or distorted thinking

ANXIETY DISORDERS:
WHEN DREAD DEBILITATES

10.   Define anxiety disorders. (559)

        For each of the anxiety disorders listed below, describe the major symptoms and possible causes for that disorder. (559-562)

        a.   panic attack disorders

                1)   symptoms

                2)   possible causes

        b.   phobias

                1)   symptoms

                2)   possible causes

        c.   obsessive-compulsive disorders

                1)   symptoms

                2)   possible causes

        d.   posttraumatic stress disorders

                1)   symptoms

                2)   possible causes

SOMATOFORM DISORDERS:
PHYSICAL SYMPTOMS WITHOUT PHYSICAL CAUSES

11.   Define somatoform disorders. (563)

Describe the major symptoms of the three somatoform disorders listed below: (563-564)

a.   somatization disorder

b.   hypochondriasis

c.   conversion disorder

There are many possible interpretations of the causes of the somatoform disorders. Describe the behavioral and cognitive interpretations. (564)

a.   behavioral explanation

b.   cognitive explanation

DISSOCIATIVE DISORDERS:
WHEN MEMORY FAILS

12.   Define dissociative disorders. (565)

Describe the major symptoms and possible causes of the two dissociative disorders listed below: (564-566)

a.   dissociative amnesia

　　1)   symptoms

　　2)   possible cause

b.   dissociative identity disorder (multiple personality)

　　1)   symptoms

　　2)   possible cause

SEXUAL AND GENDER IDENTITY DISORDERS

13.   Sexual dysfunctions are caused by disturbances in **desire**, and **arousal**. Describe the differences between sexual desire disorders and sexual arousal disorders by defining each. (567)

a.   sexual desire disorders

b.   sexual arousal disorders

Paraphilias involve unusual images, acts, or objects, which are required for sexual arousal or fulfillment. Describe the paraphilias listed below. (567-568)

a.   fetish

b.   pedophilia

c.   sexual sadism

d.   sexual masochism

e.   exhibitionism

f.   voyeurism

g.   transvestic fetishism

EATING DISORDERS

14.   Describe two eating disorders. (568-569)

a.

b.

Describe a causative factor the eating disorders share. (569)

PERSONALITY DISORDERS:
TRAITS THAT PROVE COSTLY

15.   List three specific personality traits found in people with personality disorders. (569)

a.

b.

c.

Describe the major symptoms of the three personality disorders listed below: (570-572)

a.   paranoid personality disorder

b.   schizoid personality disorder

c.   antisocial personality disorder

SCHIZOPHRENIA: OUT OF TOUCH WITH REALITY

16.   Define schizophrenia. (573)

Describe the basic nature of schizophrenia by listing and describing five types of disturbances. (574-575)

a.

b.

c.

d.

e.

Explain the difference between delusions and hallucinations. (574)

List and describe the subtypes of schizophrenia. (576)

a.

b.

c.

After reading pages 576-579, what conclusion can be reached about the cause of schizophrenia based on systematic research. In your answer include information about the five factors thought to play a role in causing schizophrenia.

17.   Describe six basic steps for preventing suicide. (580)

   a.

   b.

   c.

   d.

   e.

   f.

CHAPTER FOURTEEN QUIZ

1.   Which of the following is not one of the characteristics of psychological disorders according to your textbook? (1)

    a.   involves patterns of behavior that are unusual or atypical.
    b.   involves behavior that is viewed as undesirable by members of a given society.
    c.   causes considerable distress for the persons involved.
    d.   involves patterns of behavior that are illegal.

2.   The perspective on psychological disorder that emphasizes the notion that psychological problems represent illnesses that can be cured through appropriate treatment is the _____ perspective. (3)

    a.   medical
    b.   psychological
    c.   behavioral
    d.   cognitive

3.   According to Freud, mental disorders arise from (4)

    a.   specific biological diseases.
    b.   defective genetic make-up.
    c.   struggles between the ego and superego.
    d.   the ego experiencing anxiety.

4.   The most widely accepted system for identifying psychological disorders is known by the acronym (6)

    a.   MMPI
    b.   DSM-IV
    c.   WISC-R
    d.   K-ABC

5.   Which of the following is true? (8)

    a.   Bipolar disorders are more common than major depressions.
    b.   Depression is more common among women than men.
    c.   Women are more likely than men to successfully complete an act of suicide.
    d.   Acts of suicide are attempted more often by men than by women.

6.   It has been proposed that depression results when levels of _____ are decreased. (9)

    a.   norepinephrine and serotonin
    b.   dopamine
    c.   acetylcholine and reserpine
    d.   cholesterol

7.   Pearl periodically experiences brief but intense periods of fear and dread that do not seem to be triggered by a specific object or event. In addition to intense feelings of terror, physical symptoms such as a pounding heart, dizziness, and trembling also occur. Pearl is most likely suffering from: (10)

    a.   phobias
    b.   panic attack disorder
    c.   generalized anxiety disorder
    d.   obsessive-compulsive disorder

8.   Lillian is unable to remember anything about the fire at her residence in which her child was killed and her husband was seriously injured. This is despite the fact that she was home at the time and escaped the fire without serious injury. Lillian's failure to remember is best interpreted as: (12)

    a.   multiple personality
    b.   psychogenic amnesia
    c.   somatoform disorder
    d.   affective disorder

9.   The general term used the describe disturbances in sexual desire, sexual arousal, or the ability to attain orgasm is: (13)

    a.   paraphilia
    b.   transsexualism
    c.   transvestism
    d.   sexual dysfunction

10.   Mark suffers from a schizophrenia characterized by silliness and incoherence. He often bursts into laughter or tears for no apparent reason and can babble on meaninglessly for extended periods of time. Mark suffers from _____ schizophrenia. (16)

    a.   disorganized
    b.   paranoid
    c.   catatonic
    d.   undifferentiated

CHAPTER 15

THERAPY:
DIMINISHING THE PAIN OF PSYCHOLOGICAL DISORDERS

1. Define psychotherapies. (586) Use text, not glossary definition.

   List the major forms of psychotherapies discussed in this chapter. (587, 590, 592, 595, 598, 602)

   a.   b.
   c.   d.
   e.   f.
   g.

PSYCHOTHERAPIES:
PSYCHOLOGICAL APPROACHES TO PSYCHOLOGICAL DISORDERS

2. Describe the two features that the psychotherapies have in common. (587)

   a.

   b.

3. Describe the assumption underlying the psychodynamic therapies. (587)

   Explain Freud's beliefs about the cause of psychological disorders. (587)

Freud felt that there were two crucial tasks necessary to relieve problems causing psychological disorders. They were: (588)

a.

b.

Coming face to face with hidden feelings and impulses is known as insight. Insight leads to _____, which is defined as:

Having been freed of repression, and having experienced abreaction, people could then direct their energies into healthy growth.

4.   Psychoanalysis is the therapy developed by Freud to help the client achieve insight. Describe the following terms which depict what happens in psychoanalysis. (588-589) Use the glossary definition.

a.   free association

b.   interpretation

c.   resistance

d.   transference

5.   Describe what most psychologists have concluded about the effectiveness of psychoanalysis. (589)

Describe how modern psychodynamic therapy differs from traditional psychoanalysis. (590)

HUMANISTIC THERAPIES: EMPHASIZING THE POSITIVE

6. In the chart below, contrast Freudian and Humanistic views about Human Nature, and about the origin of psychological disorders. (590)

	FREUDIAN VIEWS	HUMANISTIC VIEWS
HUMAN NATURE		
PSYCHOLOGICAL DISORDERS		

7. Humanistic therapies include person-centered (also known as client-centered therapy) and Gestalt therapy. Describe the nature of client-centered therapy. (590-591; Fig 5.2a)

Describe Perls' explanation for psychological difficulties. (591)

List the goal of Gestalt therapy. (591)

List the three beliefs shared by Humanistic psychotherapies. (591-592)

a.

b.

c.

BEHAVIOR THERAPIES:
PSYCHOLOGICAL DISORDERS AND FAULTY LEARNING

8.   Behavior therapies share a belief that psychological disorders stem from faulty
      learning. Describe how this faulty learning develops. (592)

      a.

      b.

      List the key task for behavior therapy. (592)

9.   List and describe three techniques used in the behavior therapies based on classical
      conditioning. (593)

      a.

      b.

      c.

      List and describe three techniques used in the behavior therapies based on operant
      conditioning. (593-594)

      a.

      b.

      c.

      Describe how modeling is used in treating psychological disorders. (594-595)

COGNITIVE THERAPIES: CHANGING DISORDERED THOUGHT

10.   Cognitive therapies include **Rational Emotive Therapy, Beck's Cognitive Therapy for Depression,** and **Constructive Cognitive Therapy,** among others. Describe the basic assumption (idea) behind cognitive therapies. (595-596)

GROUP THERAPIES:
WORKING WITH OTHERS TO SOLVE PERSONAL PROBLEMS

11.   Describe the following forms of group therapy: (598-600)

       a.   psychodrama

       b.   assertiveness training

       c.   encounter or sensitivity training groups

       d.   self-help groups

       Describe the beneficial effects of subliminal self-help tapes. (600-602)

THERAPIES FOCUSED ON INTERPERSONAL RELATIONS:
MARITAL AND FAMILY THERAPY

12.   Describe the assumption underlying therapies focusing on interpersonal relations. (602)

13.   Describe the two factors which disrupt marital relationships. (603)

       a.

       b.

       Describe two goals of marital or couple therapy which attempt to deal with the disruptive factors you listed above. (603)

       a.

       b.

14.   Describe a possible assumption, made by family therapists, regarding the cause of psychological problems and for relapses experienced when a hospitalized individual returns home. (603-604)

        Describe the goals of family therapy. (604)

        In structural family therapy, the therapist works to gain insight into family relationships which lead to repeated family patterns. What is the conclusion your author reaches concerning the promising new approach known as family therapy. (604)

15.   People are often concerned as to whether or not psychotherapy is effective. Describe Eysenck's 1952 conclusion on the effectiveness of psychotherapy. (606)

        Describe the results of the following studies. (606-608)

        a.   Smith, Glass and Miller (1980)*

        b.   Orlinsky and Howard (1987)*

        c.   Robinson, Berman, and Neimeyer (1990)*

        You will not be held responsible for the names and dates, but you should know the results of the research.

16.   Research indicates that all types of psychotherapy seem to be equally effective. One
       possible reason is that all psychotherapies have elements in common. Describe the
       four elements common to all types of psychotherapy. (608-609)

       a.

       b.

       c.

       d.

       Describe how the themes of hope and personal control effect the success of therapy.

17.   Cultural bias, in terms of an individuals's race, sex, ethnic background and social
       class, plays a role in the diagnosis of abnormal behaviors. Describe four major
       changes needed to make psychotherapy more culturally sensitive. (610)

       a.

       b.

       c.

       d.

BIOLOGICALLY BASED THERAPIES

18.   Define biologically based therapies. (611)

       ECT and psychosurgery are two types of biological therapy. Describe ECT and
       Psychosurgery. (612-613 use glossary)

       a.   ECT

       b.   psychosurgery

19.   The number of hospitalized mental patients has dropped dramatically between 1955 and 1975. Some people attribute this to politics, or the economics of hospitalization. Describe what your text claims is the reason for this dramatic decline. (613)

After reading pages 613-616, complete the chart below:

Major classes of drugs	Antipsychotic drugs	Antidepressant drugs	Antianxiety drugs	Lithium
Also known as		tricyclics MAO inhibitors		Lithium
Disorders treated by these drugs			anxiety reactions phobias obsessive-compulsive disorders	
Trade name	Thorazine			Lithium carbonate
Potential side effects				

THE SETTING FOR THERAPY:
FROM INSTITUTIONAL CARE TO THE COMMUNITY

20.   Discuss the overall conclusions about the effectiveness of child abuse prevention programs for women identified to be at risk for child abuse. (Wolfe et al 1921) (618-619)

Explain whether the child abuse preventive program was an example of primary, secondary, or tertiary prevention. (618-619)

21.   List the points one should consider when choosing a therapist. (619-620)

    a.

    b.

        1)

        2)

        3)

    c.

    d.

        1)

        2)

        3)

CHAPTER FIFTEEN QUIZ

1.   Freud suggested that psychological disorders stem from the _____ of id impulses. (3)

   a.   interpretation
   b.   repression
   c.   transference
   d.   abreaction

2.   Which of the following is not one of the characteristics of psychoanalysis? (4)

   a.   dream interpretation
   b.   free association
   c.   transference
   d.   reactance

3.   Therapies based on the principles of learning are (8)

   a.   person-centered therapies
   b.   psychoanalytic therapies
   c.   Gestalt therapies
   d.   behavioral therapies

4.   Which of the following is <u>not</u> a case of applying operant conditioning principles to therapy? (9)

   a.   behavioral contracting
   b.   token economies
   c.   shaping
   d.   attribution therapy

5.   The basic assumption underlying cognitive therapies is that psychological disorders stem from (10)

   a.   faulty modes of thought
   b.   repressed impulses
   c.   biological causes
   d.   faulty learning

6.   The type of therapy that tries to understand relationships in the family is: (14)

   a.   experiential family therapy
   b.   structural family therapy
   c.   transactional analysis
   d.   encounter groups

7.   As for the effectiveness of different forms of therapy, it has been found that (15)

    a.   they are effective only with many sessions
    b.   the number of sessions has little effect
    c.   they are similarly effective
    d.   they are very different in their effectiveness

8.   Perhaps a reason why psychotherapy generally succeeds is that it gives individuals confidence that they can accomplish a variety of tasks. The term(s) that refer(s) to this type of confidence is (16)

    a.   insight and abreaction
    b.   transference
    c.   hope and personal control
    d.   therapeutic alliance

9.   The biological therapy beneficial to persons suffering from depression is (18)

    a.   electroconvulsive shock
    b.   prefrontal lobotomy
    c.   tractomies
    d.   rolfing

10.   The drugs used in treating schizophrenia are: (19)

    a.   lithium
    b.   minor tranquilizers
    c.   major tranquilizers
    d.   MAO inhibitors

CHAPTER 16

SOCIAL THOUGHT AND SOCIAL BEHAVIOR

SOCIAL THOUGHT: THINKING ABOUT OTHER PEOPLE

The process we use to figure out why other people behave the way they do is called attribution.

1.   We sometimes attribute the behavior of others to internal causes and sometimes to external causes. Describe both internal and external attribution and give an example of each. (627)

   a.   internal attribution

      example

   b.   external attribution

      example

2.   Kelley's theory of attribution tries to explain when we attribute the behavior of others to either internal or external causes. Identify and describe the three types of information Kelley thinks we use in making that decision. (627)

   a.

   b.

   c.

   Under what conditions would we be most likely to attribute another person's behavior to internal or to external causes? (627 and see Figure 16.1)

   a.   internal

   b.   external

3.   When are we most likely to use the information emphasized by Kelley? (628)

4.   Psychologists use the word "dispositional" to refer to internal causes and the word "situational" to refer to external causes. Using these two terms, describe the fundamental attribution error and give an example that is not found in your text. (629)

        a.   fundamental attribution error

        b.   example

      Is the fundamental attribution error strengthened or weakened over time?

5.   Describe self-serving bias, and give an example that is not found in your text. (630)

        a.   self-serving bias

        b.   example

      Describe how the self-serving bias can cause interpersonal friction. (630)

6.   Define social cognition. (630)

7.   Define the false consensus effect. (631)

        Describe the availability heuristic and the role it plays in the false consensus effect.
        (631)

8.   Describe counterfactual thinking and supply an example not found in your text. (633-
        634)

        a.   counterfactual thinking

        b.   example

9.   Define attitudes. (635)

        Describe three ways attitudes are formed. (636)

        a.

        b.

        c.

10.   Psychologists studying persuasion, or attitude change, look at three basic elements of
       communication: (1) the source or communicator, (2) the message, and (3) the
       audience. Summarize six of their most important research findings on persuasion.
       (636)

       a.

       b.

       c.

       d.

       e.

       f.

       Describe the elaboration likelihood model (ELM) (using the definition found in the text -
       not the definition found on the far side of the page). Also describe how and when
       messages take the central route or the peripheral route. (637 and see Figure 16.4)

       a.   elaboration likelihood model (ELM)

       b.   central route

       c.   peripheral route

11.   Describe cognitive dissonance. (638-639 and see Figure 16.5)

      Describe forced compliance, a potential cause of cognitive dissonance. (638)

      List two ways to reduce dissonance caused by forced compliance. (639)

      a.

      b.

12.   Describe the less-leads-to-more effect and include how it relates to cognitive dissonance. (639-640, and see Figure 16.6)

      Define hypocrisy and describe the experiment that demonstrated that making people aware of their own hypocrisy can change attitudes and behavior. (641-642 and see Figure 6.7)

      a.   hypocrisy

      b.   experiment

SOCIAL BEHAVIOR: INTERACTING WITH OTHERS

13.   Define prejudice. (643)

Your text discusses four potential causes of prejudice. List and describe each one. Include in your description specifically how each is likely to cause prejudice. (643-644)

   a.

   b.

   c.

   d.

14.   Psychologists study ways of reducing or preventing prejudice. Often people are not aware of their prejudices, and until they are made aware, they are not able to counteract them. Describe how teachers can play a role in reducing prejudice. (645)

15.   Define the contact hypothesis. (645)

Describe five situations in which intergroup contact is likely to reduce prejudice. (645-646)

a.

b.

c.

d.

e.

16.   Define recategorization. (646)

Describe the relationship some researchers have found between recategorization and prejudice. (646)

17. List and describe the three components of racial identification. (647 and see Figure 16.8)

   a.

   b.

   c.

   Describe the relationship between racial identification and personal experience with racial prejudice for African Americans. (648)

   Discuss some outcomes of strong racial identification. (648-649)

18. Define conformity. (649)

   Define social norms. (649)

   Give an example of a situation in which conformity is useful and a situation in which conformity is not useful. (649)

   a.   useful

   b.   not useful

19.   Describe Asch's study on conformity. Include in your description the percentage of people who conformed at least once. (650)

Describe the relationship of conformity to group size. (650-651)

Describe the effect that having an ally has on conformity. (651)

20.   Compliance involves one person asking another to change his or her behavior in a way that the requester wants. Describe five different tactics that seem to be effective in gaining compliance, and give an example of each. (653-654)

    a.   ingratiation

        example

    b.   foot-in-the-door approach

        example

c.   door-in-the-face approach

example

d.   that's not all approach

example

e.   complaining

example

21.   Define obedience. (655)

Describe Milgram's laboratory simulation of obedience. Include in your description the percentage of subjects who showed total obedience. (655-656 and see Figure 16.12)

Describe three factors or situations which help explain why many persons are so willing to yield to the commands of sources of authority. (657-658)

a.

b.

c.

Describe three factors or situations which are likely to decrease obedience. (658)

a.

b.

c.

22.   Define prosocial behavior. (658)

Define the bystander effect. (660)

Describe diffusion of responsibility. (660)

List and describe two other factors that play an important role in determining whether or not victims will receive aid. (660-661)

a.

b.

23.   Define interpersonal attraction. (662)

List and describe four factors that play an important role in understanding interpersonal attraction. (662-664)

a.

b.

c.

d.

24.   Define romantic love. (664)

Describe the three basic conditions necessary for a person to conclude that he/she is in love. (664)

a.

b.

c.

List and describe two biochemical reactions sometimes experienced by people in love. (665)

a.

b.

List and describe four factors that can weaken romantic relationships over time. (665-666)

a.

b.

c.

d.

25.   Define environmental psychology. (667)

Describe the relationship between temperature and aggression found by researchers in laboratory studies. (667)

CHAPTER SIXTEEN QUIZ

1. The basic task in making a causal attribution is to determine if a behavior is caused by: (1)

    a.   consensus or consistency
    b.   internal or external causes
    c.   objective or subjective causes
    d.   consistency or distinctiveness

2. Kelley suggests that we are most likely to attribute another's behavior to internal causes when: (2)

    a.   consistency and consensus are high, and distinctiveness is low.
    b.   consensus and distinctiveness are low, and consistency is high.
    c.   consensus and distinctiveness are high, and consistency is low.
    d.   consistency and consensus are low, and distinctiveness is high.

3. The tendency to take credit for our positive behaviors by attributing them to internal causes and to blame negative ones on external causes is called the: (5)

    a.   fundamental attribution error
    b.   self-monitoring bias
    c.   automatic vigilance
    d.   self-serving bias

4. Thinking that most people are in favor of legalizing drugs, as you are, is most likely an example of: (7)

    a.   false consensus effect
    b.   self-serving bias
    c.   prosocial behavior
    d.   social norms

5. The prediction that negative outcomes that follow unusual behavior will generate more sympathy for the persons who experience them than negative outcomes that follow usual or typical behavior is based on: (8)

    a.   diffusion of responsibility
    b.   motivated skepticism
    c.   counterfactual thinking
    d.   fundamental attribution

6. Which of the following speakers is most likely to change the attitude of members of an audience? (10)

    a.   one who speaks at a faster than normal rate
    b.   one who speaks at a slower than normal rate
    c.   one who speaks at a normal rate
    d.   none of the other alternatives, since the rate of speaking has no influence on attitude change.

7.   The uncomfortable state we experience when there is an unpleasant gap between our attitudes and our actions is called: (11)

        a.   self-denial
        b.   counterfactual thinking
        c.   cognitive dissonance
        d.   false consensus effect

8.   Negative attitudes toward the members of specific social groups based solely on their membership in that group is called: (13)

        a.   discrimination
        b.   racial identification
        c.   prejudice
        d.   stereotypes

9.   According to the contact hypothesis, which of the following proposals for Hispanic and Anglo third graders is best designed to help reduce prejudice between the two groups? (15)

        a.   Gifted Hispanic students tutor Anglo students having problem in mathematics.
        b.   Hispanic and Anglo students attend a formal lecture on the virtues of world cooperation.
        c.   Hispanic and Anglo students work together on organizing a school recycling program.
        d.   Hispanic and Anglo students individually write essays on why people need to share with each other.

10.   After friends help you move your entertainment center you immediately ask them to help you paint your living room. This is an example of what social psychologists call: (20)

        a.   foot-in-the-door approach
        b.   automatic vigilance
        c.   forced compliance
        d.   planting the seed

CHAPTER 17

PSYCHOLOGY GOES TO WORK:
INDUSTRIAL/ORGANIZATIONAL PSYCHOLOGY AND HUMAN FACTORS

1.   Describe the focus of industrial/organizational psychology. (676)

       List some examples of issues examined in this field. (676)

       a.

       b.

       c.

       d.

       Describe human factors.

       List three areas in which these subfields overlap. (676)

       a.

       b.

       c.

INDUSTRIAL/ORGANIZATIONAL PSYCHOLOGY: THE SYSTEMATIC STUDY OF BEHAVIOR IN WORK SETTINGS

2. Psychologists are interested in the question of how you best motivate people to work hard at their jobs. Expectancy theory, goal-setting theory, and equity theory have been proposed to help us understand these issues. Describe the general focus and key aspects of each theory, then make up or report a real life example of each one.

a. Expectancy Theory (678 and see figure 17.1)

   1) general focus

   2) key aspects

      a)

      b)

      c)

   3) example

b. Goal-Setting Theory (678-680 and see figure 17.2)

   1) general focus

   2) reasons goal-setting affects performance

      a)

      b)

      c)

   3) example

c.   Equity Theory (680-682 and see figure 17.3)

1)   general focus

2)   key aspects

a)   social comparison

b)   inequity

c)   ways that feelings of inequity interfere with work motivation

(1)

(2)

(3)

3)   Describe a recent study of how feelings of inequity affected the performance of professional basketball players.

3.   In addition to generating theories and research, Industrial/Organizational psychologists are devising practical ways to increase motivation in the workplace. List and describe the four methods discussed in your text. (682-683 and 685)

a.

b.

c.

d.

4.   Describe computer-based work monitoring and summarize it's advantages and disadvantages in relation to simple and complex tasks. (685-686)

    a.   computer-based work monitoring

    b.   advantages

    c.   disadvantages

    d.   Would your work performance be improved under this system? Why or why not?

5.   Performance appraisal, evaluating the performance of others, is a very important, yet a very difficult task. Describe the following sources of error in performance appraisal. (686-689)

    a.   errors in attribution

    b.   halo effects

    c.   leniency errors

    d.   stereotypes

6.   Describe how gender stereotypes affect employment opportunities. (690 and see Figure 17.5)

7.   Accuracy of performance appraisals can be increased. Describe the following procedures.

     a.   Accurate Records: Describe the procedure for keeping complete and accurate diary notes. (691-692)

     b.   Describe three respects in which diary notes are valuable. (692)

          1)

          2)

          3)

     c.   Rating Formats: Sometimes the form of the evaluation can influence its accuracy. Describe two major rating scale formats. (692-694)

          1)

          2)

8.   In terms of hiring employees, gender stereotyping is often a significant issue. Describe how gender stereotypes compare to traits often viewed as necessary for success in high level jobs. (690)

Describe how the impact of gender stereotypes can be reduced. (691)

9.   The term job satisfaction refers to the positive or negative attitudes people hold toward their jobs. Psychologists have found job satisfaction to be a relatively stable trait - maybe even a genetic one. However, there is evidence that job satisfaction is influenced by external as well as internal factors. Describe five work related influences on job satisfaction. (695-696)

a.

b.

c.

d.

e.

Describe three person-related influences on job satisfaction. (696)

a.

b.

c.

10.   Industrial/Organizational psychologists find that leaders actually do differ from other persons in several important - and measurable - respects. List and understand eight traits that contribute to leaders' success. (700-701 and see Table 17.3)

     a.

     b.

     c.

     d.

     e.

     f.

     g.

     h.

Describe how flexibility plays an important role in leadership situations. (700)

11.   List and describe two theories of leader effectiveness and include the importance of flexibility to each theory. (701)

     a.

     b.

12.   Describe charismatic leaders. (702)

List four special traits charismatic leaders possess that influence their followers. (702)

   a.

   b.

   c.

   d.

List four common reactions of followers to charismatic leaders. (702)

   a.

   b.

   c.

   d.

13.   List and describe the three essential factors of charismatic leadership. (702-703)

   a.

   b.

   c.

HUMAN FACTORS:
DESIGNING FOR EFFECTIVENESS AND SAFETY

14.   State the guiding principle of the field of Human Factors. (703)

15.   Describe five important principles in the visual presentation of information. (704)

     a.

     b.

     c.

     d.

     e.

16.   List and describe four methods for increasing the effectiveness of warnings so that people
        will notice and comply with them. (705-706)

        a.

        b.

        c.

        d.

17.   Describe some important considerations in the design of controls. (706-708)

        a.   compatibility

        b.   predictor displays

        c.   supervisory control

18.   Describe six procedures organizations can follow to maximize office layouts. (712)

a.

b.

c.

d.

e.

f.

MAKING PSYCHOLOGY PART OF YOUR LIFE

19.   List and describe six ways to increase your chances of making a good impression on a
       job interview. (712-713)

a.

b.

c.

d.

e.

f.

CHAPTER SEVENTEEN QUIZ

1. A subfield of psychology that focuses on all aspects of behavior in work settings and on the nature of work settings themselves is: (1)

    a. industrial/organizational psychology
    b. human factors psychology
    c. employment psychology
    d. career counseling psychology

2. According to the goal-setting theory of work motivation, an individual's motivation to work will increase if the goals set are: (2)

    a. challenging
    b. general and not very specific
    c. set on the basis of economic goals and not workers' beliefs
    d. as described in all the other alternatives

3. Tending to evaluate almost everything a person does as favorable because we have a favorable impression of the individual is an example of: (5)

    a. fundamental attribution error
    b. leniency effect
    c. normative thinking effect
    d. halo effect

4. One of the most important characteristics of leadership is the capacity to recognize and adopt the actions or style of leadership which are required in a given situation. This capacity is called: (10)

    a. flexibility
    b. autocracy
    c. self-confidence
    d. leadership motivation

5. Research suggests that charismatic leaders do <u>all but</u> one of the following: (13)

    a. motivate followers through fear tactics
    b. possess and transmit a vision of the future
    c. give meaning and purpose to the actions they request
    d. offer a clear road map for attaining the visions they promote

6. Which of the following is <u>not</u> a basic principle of visual display design? (15)

    a. Pointers moving against a fixed scale are harder to read than the opposite.
    b. Gradation in scale should be clear and easy to read.
    c. Use clockwise directions to indicate increments in scale.
    d. Different colors should be used for different zones.

7.   Which of the following increases the effectiveness of warnings? (16)

    a.   only interactive warnings
    b.   only personalized warnings
    c.   both interactive and personalized warnings
    d.   neither interactive nor personalized warnings

8.   The degree to which controls operate in a manner consistent with human expectations is called: (17)

    a.   human factors.
    b.   expectancy theory
    c.   predictability
    d.   compatibility

9.   Which of the following interpersonal aspects of workspace design is preferred by most people? (18)

    a.   designs which promote uniformity
    b.   designs which minimize privacy
    c.   designs which allow for personalization
    d.   designs which separate higher-status persons

10.   Which of the following is considered to be appropriate for a successful interview? (19)

    a.   demonstrating basic knowledge of the company for which you are interviewed
    b.   occasional self-deprecating remarks
    c.   standard business attire for the interview
    d.   All of the other alternatives are appropriate for a successful interview.

APPENDIX

STATISTICS:
USES—AND POTENTIAL ABUSES

1. In order to understand the meaning of the results obtained in their research, psychologists use statistics. Define statistics. (716)

2. Statistics can be used for many different purposes. List the four tasks which can be accomplished by using statistics. (716)

    a.

    b.

    c.

    d.

DESCRIPTIVE STATISTICS: SUMMARIZING DATA

3. Before data is summarized, it is often arranged into a frequency distribution. Describe what kind of information is obtained through the use of a frequency distribution. (717)

4. Describe how each of the following measures of central tendency is calculated. (717-718)

    a. mean

    b. median

    c. mode

NOTE - While the mode, the most frequently occurring score, is also a possible measure of central tendency, it is actually used very rarely. It is possible to have none, or more than one mode in any distribution.

5. As implied by its name, descriptive statistics are used to describe (or summarize) the major characteristics of a set of scores obtained through some kind of measurement. Describe what each of the following types of descriptive statistics attempts to measure. (717-718)

    a.   measures of central tendency

    b.   measures of dispersion

6. The simplest measure of dispersion is the range. How is the range calculated? (718-719)

    The most useful measure of dispersion is the standard deviation. What does the standard deviation represent? (719)

    Complete the following statements about the standard deviation. (719)

    a.   The _____ the standard deviation, the more the scores are spread out from the center of the distribution.

    b.   The _____ the standard deviation, the less the scores are spread out from the center of the distribution.

7. The normal curve describes the way in which scores are distributed for an amazingly wide range of human characteristics. Complete the following statements about the normal curve. (719-720; and see Figure A.2)

    a.   The normal curve is a symmetrical, _____ - _____ frequency distribution.

    b.   In a normal curve, most scores are found near the _____ and fewer and fewer scores occur toward the _____.

    c.   Draw a normal curve in the space below.

Once we know the mean of a normal distribution and its standard deviation, we can determine the relative standing of any specific score within it. Complete the following statements about scores in a normal distribution. (720-721; and see Figure A.3)

a.   _____% of all scores in a normal distribution fall above the mean and _____% of the scores will fall below the mean.

b.   _____% of all scores in a normal distribution will fall between the mean and one standard deviation above or below the mean.

c.   68% of all scores in a normal distribution will fall between _____ standard deviation above the mean and _____ standard deviation below the mean.

d.   _____% of all scores in a normal distribution will fall between two standard deviations below the mean and two standard deviations above the mean.

e.   If a score falls two standard deviations above the mean in a normal distribution, only _____% of all scores are equal to or higher than that score.

NOTE: In a normal curve, if a score is one standard deviation above the mean, 84% of all scores will fall below that point. We know that 50% of the scores fall below the mean and that 34% of the scores will fall between the mean and one standard deviation above the mean. We add these two figures to arrive at 84%.

INFERENTIAL STATISTICS: DETERMINING WHETHER DIFFERENCES ARE OR ARE NOT REAL

8.   Define inferential statistics. (721)

When a researcher applies inferential statistics to the interpretation of differences between groups obtained in psychological research, that researcher makes a very conservative assumption. Describe this assumption. (722)

NOTE: In ordinary psychological practice, a difference between groups is considered to be significant (or real) only if the likelihood of these differences occurring by chance is 5% or less. In many of the studies described in your text, the differences obtained between groups as a result of experimental procedures were so large that they would have occurred by chance fewer than one time in every hundred (1%).

CORRELATION AND PREDICTION

9.   Psychologists are often interested in whether scores on two variables are <u>related</u> to each other. Remember, this is quite different than asking whether changes in one variable <u>cause</u> changes in another variable. After reading the material in your textbook on correlation, complete the following statements. (723)

a.   To obtain a precise index of the strength of a relationship between two or more variables, we often calculate a statistic known as the _____ _____.

b.   These correlation coefficients can range from _____ to _____.

c.   A positive correlation indicates that as scores on one variable increase, the scores on the other variable also _____. A negative correlation indicates that as scores on one variable increase, the scores on the other variable _____.

d.   The greater the number from 0.00 toward +1.00 or -1.00, the _____ is the relationship between scores on the two variables.

e.   Once we have computed a correlation coefficient, we can determine whether it is significant. That is, we can determine whether it is large enough to be viewed as unlikely to have occurred as a result of _____.

NOTE: Refer back to Chapter One, learning objective #12, to review the three advantages of the correlational method of research.

THE MISUSE OF STATISTICS: NUMBERS DON'T LIE ... OR DO THEY?

10.   Statistics can sometimes be misused to confuse, deceive, or mislead us. After reading the textbook material about how this can occur, complete the following statements. (724-727)

a.   Even events that would be expected to occur by chance very rarely do actually occur. Therefore, **don't** overinterpret events that seem to border on impossible. They may actually be _____ occurrences with no special significance of their own.

b.   Be _____ of claims based on very small samples. They are on shaky grounds, and they may be designed to be purposely misleading.

c.   Surveys are meaningless if the people surveyed represent a biased sample and are not representative of the general population. Thus it is important to always ask about any survey, 1) _____ were the persons surveyed, and 2) how were they _____?

d.   Whenever you are told that a product, a candidate, or anything else is better or superior in some way, always ask the question: better than _____?

e.   Assume that all differences reported in advertisements and similar sources are not
_____ - that is, not real - unless specific information to the
contrary is provided.

f.   Graphs may be used to distort reality. When viewing graphs it is important to pay
careful attention to the _____ used in the graph, to the precise
_____ being measured, and to all of the _____
employed in the graph.

APPENDIX QUIZ

1. Which of the following is <u>not</u> an important use of statistics in psychological research? (2)

    a. describing data
    b. gathering data
    c. interpreting data
    d. predicting future behavior

2. Scores on a 10-point quiz for 10 students are distributed like so: 4, 4, 4, 5, 6, 6, 7, 7, 7, and 10. The median of this distribution is: (4)

    a. 4
    b. 5
    c. 6
    d. 7

3. Measures of central tendency are _____ statistics. (5)

    a. inferential
    b. predictive
    c. correlational
    d. descriptive

4. The larger the _____, the more the scores are spread out from the center of the distribution. (6)

    a. range
    b. mode
    c. standard deviation
    d. median

5. The symmetrical, bell-shaped frequency distribution in which most scores are found near the middle with fewer and fewer scores occurring toward the extremes is called the: (7)

    a. Simons distribution
    b. normal curve
    c. inferential curve
    d. descriptive distribution

6. The distribution of scores on Owana's test of fashion design is a normal one. The mean is 100 and the standard deviation is 20. Therefore, 68% of the scores on this test fall between: (7)

    a. 90 and 100
    b. 60 and 140
    c. 85 and 125
    d. 80 and 120

7. _____ statistics are used to determine whether experimental findings are "real" or "chance." (8)

    a.   Descriptive
    b.   Inferential
    c.   Central
    d.   Hypothetical

8. Which of the following could not be a correlation coefficient? (9)

    a.   +1.12
    b.   -.56
    c.   +.68
    d.   neither A nor B could be correlation coefficients

9. Assume that a researcher has found a strong negative correlation between two variables. A strong negative correlation means that: (9)

    a.   there is no relationship between the two variables
    b.   persons who obtain high scores on the first variable also tend to obtain high scores on the second variable
    c.   persons who obtain high scores on the first variable tend to obtain low scores on the second variable
    d.   persons who obtain low scores on the first variable also tend to obtain low scores on the second variable

10. Be skeptical of claims based on _____ samples because they are on very shaky statistical ground. (10)

    a.   small
    b.   large
    c.   random
    d.   representative

ANSWER KEY

Chapter 1
1. d   2. b   3. c   4. d   5. c   6. a   7. c   8. d   9. b   10. c

Chapter 2
1. d   2. d   3. c   4. a   5. c   6. c   7. d   8. b   9. d   10. b

Chapter 3
1. d   2. a   3. b   4. b   5. c   6. d   7. b   8. a   9. a   10. d

Chapter 4
1. d   2. d   3. b   4. a   5. a   6. d   7. c   8. b   9. c   10. c

Chapter 5
1. c   2. d   3. b   4. d   5. c   6. d   7. b   8. b   9. a   10. d

Chapter 6
1. b   2. a   3. a   4. a   5. c   6. a   7. c   8. b   9. d   10. c

Chapter 7
1. d   2. c   3. d   4. c   5. a   6. c   7. d   8. c   9. b   10. a

Chapter 8
1. d   2. c   3. c   4. b   5. b   6. c   7. b   8. d   9. c   10. c

Chapter 9
1. a   2. d   3. a   4. a   5. d   6. a   7. d   8. b   9. c   10. d

Chapter 10
1. a   2. d   3. b   4. c   5. d   6. a   7. d   8. b   9. b   10. b

Chapter 11
1. d   2. b   3. c   4. a   5. d   6. c   7. c   8. c   9. b   10. c

Chapter 12
1. c   2. b   3. d   4. a   5. b   6. b   7. d   8. c   9. c   10. c

Chapter 13
1. b   2. d   3. c   4. d   5. a   6. d   7. d   8. c   9. c   10. b

Chapter 14
1. d   2. a   3. d   4. b   5. b   6. a   7. b   8. b   9. d   10. a

Chapter 15
1. b   2. d   3. d   4. d   5. a   6. b   7. c   8. c   9. a   10. c

Chapter 16
1. b   2. b   3. d   4. a   5. c   6. a   7. c   8. c   9. c   10. a

Chapter 17
1. a   2. a   3. d   4. a   5. a   6. a   7. c   8. d   9. c   10. d

Appendix
1. b   2. c   3. d   4. c   5. b   6. d   7. b   8. a   9. c   10. a